Roberts Dorothea

Two Royal Lives Gleanings from Berlin and from the Lives of Their Imperial Highnesses

The Crown Prince and Princess of Germany

Roberts Dorothea

Two Royal Lives Gleanings from Berlin and from the Lives of Their Imperial Highnesses
The Crown Prince and Princess of Germany

ISBN/EAN: 9783337320362

Printed in Europe, USA, Canada, Australia, Japan

Cover: Foto ©ninafisch / pixelio.de

More available books at **www.hansebooks.com**

TWO ROYAL LIVES

GLEANINGS FROM BERLIN AND FROM THE LIVES OF

THEIR IMPERIAL HIGHNESSES

THE CROWN PRINCE AND PRINCESS OF GERMANY

BY

DOROTHEA ROBERTS

WITH PORTRAITS

Fifth Edition.

> "And so these twain, upon the skirts of Time,
> Sit side by side, full summed in all their powers,
> Dispensing harvest, sowing the To-be,
> Self-reverent each, and reverencing each,
> Distinct in individualities,
> But like each other ev'n as those who love."
> —*The Princess.*

London

T. FISHER UNWIN

26 Paternoster Square

MDCCCLXXXVIII

LIST OF ILLUSTRATIONS.

MEDALLION PORTRAITS OF T. R. I. H. THE CROWN PRINCE AND PRINCESS OF GERMANY	*Frontispiece*	
H. R. I. H. THE CROWN PRINCE OF GERMANY	*Facing page*	11
H. R. I. H. THE CROWN PRINCESS OF GERMANY	,,	53
H. R. I. H. PRINCE WILLIAM . .	,,	113
THE VICTORIA BARRACK, HOMBOURG .	,,	149
INTERIOR OF THE VICTORIA BARRACK	,,	157
H. R. I. H. PRINCESS WILLIAM . .	,,	165
T. R. I. H. PRINCE WILLIAM, PRINCE FREDERICK, PRINCE ADALBERT	,,	179
LITTLE ARCHITECTS . . .	,,	235
THE BATH-ROOM	,,	249
LITTLE LAUNDRESSES . . .	,,	259
LITTLE MUSICIANS	,,	261

CONTENTS.

CHAPTER I.
INTRODUCTORY ... ... PAGE 1

CHAPTER II.
BOYHOOD OF PRINCE FREDERICK WILLIAM (1831-1850) 11

CHAPTER III.
PRINCE FREDERICK WILLIAM VISITS ENGLAND (1850-1855) 23

CHAPTER IV.
BETROTHAL OF PRINCE FREDERICK WILLIAM (1855-1858) 37

CHAPTER V.
CHILDHOOD OF THE PRINCESS ROYAL (1841–1847)   53

CHAPTER VI.
GIRLHOOD OF THE PRINCESS ROYAL (1847–1858)   67

CHAPTER VII.
THE ROYAL MARRIAGE (JAN. THE 25TH, 1858) ... 85

CHAPTER VIII.
WELCOME TO BERLIN (FEB. THE 8TH, 1858) ... 97

CHAPTER IX.
THE DARKNESS AND THE DAWN (1859–1863) 113

CHAPTER X.
SEVEN YEARS OF WAR (1864–1871) 133

CHAPTER XI.
THE WOMEN OF GERMANY DURING THE FRANCO-GERMAN WAR (1870–1871) 149

CHAPTER XII.
SEVEN YEARS OF PEACE (1871–1878) 165

CONTENTS.

CHAPTER XIII.
GRIEF AND JOY IN THE ROYAL HOME (1878-1886) ... 179

CHAPTER XIV.
ART AND INDUSTRY IN BERLIN 197

CHAPTER XV.
SERVANTS OF THE SICK POOR 217

CHAPTER XVI.
THE CHILD'S GARDEN AND ITS PROMOTERS ... 235

CHAPTER XVII.
THE PESTALOZZI-FRÖBEL HOUSE 251

PREFACE.

When the Silver Wedding of the Imperial Prince and Princess of Germany was celebrated in 1888, many Lives of both those royal personages appeared in the Fatherland. One of these books found its way to England, was favourably reviewed by our newspapers, and was offered to me for translation; but as it proved, on perusal, to be chiefly compiled from English sources, the project was soon laid aside.

I chanced to mention the suggestion some time afterwards to a gentleman familiar with German life and literature as well as with German modes of thinking—" But," said he, " would it not be well if the people of England could know more about the future rulers of the great German Empire, and the efforts they are so constantly making for the good of their fellow men? Would it not be stimulating, and in many ways instructive, to discover how full of *hard and earnest work* the lives of princes often are? Would it not be well to make the people of this country aware of the high value which the Germans set upon the English alliance, as well as of the cordial relations now existing in the Fatherland between Princes and People?"

Though impressed by my friend's words, it was not until I had seen some of the beneficent work he referred to that I could feel justified in attempting the record then suggested. Nor was it without many misgivings as to my fitness for the task that, after two visits to Berlin, this little book was commenced, for however delightful it might be to trace the course of those royal lives, and to speak of the noble institutions which embody their aims and aspirations, I could scarcely hope that an earnest purpose would atone for lack of literary skill and experience.

As space would admit of but few details, I have aimed at presenting one or two descriptive pictures in each chapter, rather than a summary of all the events included in the period referred to. In this purpose I have been aided by the lively accounts of many German writers, extracts from whose works may lend value to the following pages.

In an odd number of *Harper's Magazine* I found by accident a long and interesting sketch of the life of the Crown Prince, written by Dr. George von Bunsen, for the information of the Americans, from which it was especially satisfactory to quote, as this gentleman, the son of the late Chevalier Bunsen is associated with the Imperial Prince and Princess in the philanthropic work of Berlin, and can speak with authority of what he knows from personal observation. I have also to thank the writers of the following books for useful facts:

PREFACE. xiii

Friedrich Wilhelm, ein Fürstenbild aus dem 19ten Jahrhundert, by Hermann Hongst (Berlin, 1883); *Die Männer der neuen deutschen Zeit*, by C. Brachvogel (Hanover, 1873); *Frauenarbeit*, by Amelie Sohr (Berlin, 1882); *Im Silberkrans*, by Elise Polko (Berlin, 1883); *Denkwürdigkeiten, aus den Papieren des Freiherrn C. F. von Stockmar* (Brunswick, 1872); *Unterhaltung am Häuslichen Herd*, Dr. G. Hinzpeter (Bielefeld, 1883); *Victoria, Kronprinzessin des deutschen Reichs*, by Lina Morgenstern (Berlin, 1883); *Early Years of the Prince Consort*, by General Sir Charles Grey (London, 1867); *Life of the Prince Consort*, by Sir Theodore Martin (London, 1875, etc.); *Leaves from the Journal of our Life in the Highlands*, edited by Sir Arthur Helps (London, 1867, etc.); *Hand-work and Head-work*, from the German of the Baroness Marenholz von Bülow (London, 1885); *Autobiography of Friedrich Fröbel*, from the German (London, 1886); *The Kindergarten, Principles of Fröbel's System*, by Miss Shirreff (London, 1880).

I have been so fortunate as to obtain the use of several photographs for the illustration of this book. The three quarter-length portraits of the Crown Prince and Crown Princess were taken during the past autumn. The plates are the property of their Imperial Highnesses, who have graciously granted permission for their reproduction here. The little groups of children at work in the Berlin *Volkskindergarten*, are taken from photographs presented to the Princess on the twenty-fifth anniversary of her wedding-day. The two reproductions of the Field-Lazareth at Hombourg, with portraits of the Princess and her suite standing outside the building, are taken from large photographs presented to Miss Florence Lees (now Mrs. Dacre Craven), when she quitted Hombourg, at the close of the Franco-German War.

PLEASLEY VALE, MANSFIELD.

I.

INTRODUCTORY.

*As man and wife, being two, are one in love,
So be there 'twixt your kingdoms such a spousal
That never may ill office or fell jealousy*

. . . . . .

Thrust in between the paction. . . .

KING HENRY V.

THERE is an ancient prophecy still current amongst the Prussian people, which promises that "great good luck will follow the marriage of the heir to the Hohenzollern throne with a Princess of the sea-girt Isle."[1]

As you wander through the quaint, small rooms of the Monbijou Palace in Berlin, used now for a Hohenzollern museum, in two of them you may observe two fair Hanoverian Princesses smiling down upon you from the walls. Each lady surveys her own workboxes, writing-tables, toilet arrangements, left just as she once used them, and one is

[1] England.

surrounded by the waxen images of her little long-dead children. The first is Sophie Charlotte, the sister of our George the First, and wife of Frederick, first King of Prussia: "A very distinguished woman," says Carlyle, "who has left some trace of herself in German culture to the present day." The second is Queen Sophie Dorothée, her niece, and the wife of her only child, that brusque and rather peremptory King, Frederick William the First, famed for his gigantic grenadiers; the mother also of fourteen little princes and princesses, of whom the Great Frederick was the fifth child and third surviving son. He, a Crown Prince Fritz of the eighteenth century, cherished for many years the hope of winning that long foretold English bride, who was to be the harbinger of good fortune to his country and his dynasty; but Hapsburg counsels prevailed, and the Prussian Prince was not suffered to wed his cousin, our Princess Amelia.

The happiness denied to his great ancestor came to a Crown Prince Fritz of a later century in quite the good, old-world fashion, no State intrigues, no rivalries or jealousies now intervening to mar the union of two young hearts and lives, and also of two great nationalities, for wherever you may turn in Berlin the bond between our two cognate nations is brought pleasantly to mind.

My friend and I once spent an interesting

morning in the arsenal, a noble building facing the royal palaces in Berlin, wondering to find how interesting arms can be made, even to the female mind, when intelligibly arranged.—" Have you got any English spoils of war here?" I ventured to inquire of a be-medaled veteran, who had just given us a vivid little *résumé* of German history, beginning with Karl der Grosse (Charlemagne), and ending with those burnished metal warriors who stand round the Ruhmeshalle hard by, their faces fixed on a celestial creature— Deutsche Treue (Fidelity)—pointing heavenwards in their midst. The good old man's eyes glistened, his voice grew soft, as he said, " Ach! No—we have guns given, not taken. If only the *gnädige* (gracious) lady could see our Frau Kronprinzessin when she comes in here, linked with her *Mann* (husband), they would know that *we* are brothers! Why, what is your very language, but just German *kauderwälscht* (barbarized German)—Ja wohl! Our Frau Kronprinzessin is much beloved by our people," he added, after a little pause.

Another day, when we visited the museum of industrial art in the Königgrätzer Strasse, we found the intelligent men in charge of each of its rooms pleased to let English visitors know how unceasingly their Princess and her husband occupy themselves with the development of that delightful place for the benefit of the working classes. When the Crown Prince opened the present beautiful building, on the birthday of the Princess, in 1881, he reminded those who were present that it "had been brought to completion by the efforts of the Crown Princess, inspired, as she is, by the same spirit which actuated her revered and ever-to-be-lamented father."

All the great public galleries and museums of the capital bear traces of the personal care which is bestowed upon them by the future rulers of the German Empire, who have strong faith in the ennobling and refining influence of art. Yet it is not in them only that we find proof of their interest in the advancement of the people, we see it still further exemplified in the numerous institutions for the training of the young, and in the beneficent societies, of various kinds, which have their active sympathy and practical support.

In Berlin there are many associations of cultivated and philanthropic men and women working silently and ceaselessly, for the improvement of their fellow-men, from the foundation of the social fabric upwards. These unsectarian and purely charitable societies have the constant help of the Crown Prince and Crown Princess, and it is of these, as illustrating their aims and motives, that I would now give a few preliminary details in connection with their lives. Those who are brought into personal relation with the future Emperor and Empress of Germany in the furtherance of educational and beneficent work tell you—speaking too with emotion—how broad and enlightened are all their views, how beneficent are their dealings with their fellow-men. They tell you how warm their interest is in all that can tend towards the progress of the human race, how just and liberal their estimate of the value of social reforms; but above all they speak of their sense of the importance of education—education, that is to say, as distinguished from mere instruction, and which implies a training of the mind and heart, a development of those finer feelings which Germans comprehend under the word *Gemüth*.

The Crown Princess conceives that this education, this trained power of perceiving divine and lovely things, may best be fostered by the association of rich and poor, gentle and simple, for their mutual good. For instance—The ladies of her Nursing Home go forth each day to tend the sick poor; they bring ease to the sufferer and relief to the hard-worked mother; but besides this, they introduce order into the home; they cleanse it with their own hands, they let in the fresh air; by their gentle ministrations they often bring moral health also to the poor household.

The tiny creature that comes from some poor cellar in Berlin to the Princess's *Volkskindergarten*, or " child's garden for the people," in the Steinmetzer Strasse, finds an educated gentlewoman waiting there to take it by the hand, to wash its little body clean herself; then to begin the harder task of cleansing its mind and spirit of all rough and cruel impulses, so that those germs of good which God has implanted in all His children may find room to grow freely. While she shows her little pupil how mutual love and helpfulness can make life bright that lady's own heart grows richer, her own life gains a new value and interest from the relations which soon grow up between "Tante" and "Kind" —auntie and child.—Kindergarten teachers are called *Tante*, or Auntie, by their children.

In our concluding chapters, I hope to describe the Pestalozzi-Fröbel House in Berlin, and the happy little world which is gathered beneath its wide roof. I should like also to give my readers a picture of the pretty Christmas festival of this infant community, when two Englishwomen were permitted to see the future Emperor and Empress of Germany the centre of an eager throng of tiny beings—the smallest and poorest of their subjects—scattering magic gifts, and still more precious words and smiles, around them.

When my friend and I had left that festive little gathering and were wending our way homewards, we said to one another—"That was indeed true kingship!"—A glow was at our hearts as we remembered that the gentle lady, with her beaming smiles and encouraging words, who had bestowed those gifts, was our countrywoman—our Princess Royal.

One afternoon a lady, known for her warm interest in all good works, had driven us to see the Friedrichshain Hospital, remodelled by the Crown Princess three years ago. The Princess had just been there. She had come, we were told, laden with gifts for old and young, to furnish forth the Christmas trees which sweet-faced lady-nurses were then busily decking in each ward. In the children's wards it was touching to see how the big wistful eyes brightened, and the cheeks flushed, when "Auntie" (the nursing sister) came up to the small white beds. A thin little hand was stretched out, a wan smile greeted even the "Auntie" from England as she went by, for the little ones in this spacious, airy room, with its birds, and flowers, and toys, have learnt from the gentle ladies who nurse them to look for nothing save love and kind offices from all who come to see them.

The Crown Princess often visits them. She takes these little sufferers into her arms and soothes and loves them. Her own great sorrows have made her pitiful towards all sick children. This mother's heart will always bleed as she thinks of her two beautiful and promising boys taken from her so suddenly long years ago. It is touching to hear that the poor people of Berlin used sometimes to leave flowers by the way, when it was known that this sorrowing mother might be passing, as she daily visited the chapel where the mortal part of her lost treasure was laid.—Such mute tokens of their sympathy might help to soothe even a mother's grief.

Our Princess of the "sea-girt Isle" does indeed endear herself more and more to the people of her adopted country, for in her they can see the inspiring and sympathetic wife and mother of their future Emperors. Her husband, the brave Hohenzollern Prince, has an unbounded popularity in the Fatherland.—"Who is there in Germany who does not know that the Crown Prince is the same *friendly gentleman* to all, without distinction of age, sex, or rank; that he uses his high station to bring peace and joy to the dwellings of rich and poor alike?" Thus confidently writes the biographer of "unser Fritz." To the Germans that affectionate cognomen means more than its literal translation implies. It means rather "our own," or "our dear Fritz," than simply "our Fritz," and it was in that sense that the South Germans used it in speaking of their young Prussian commander during the time of the last great war.

The Crown Princess has been called "one of the most distinguished women in Europe." She is distinguished not merely by virtue of her high and responsible position, but by her talents, by her enthusiasm for all wise and righteous reforms, and by the same clear judgment and sound sense which characterized her father, the Prince Consort. Speaking of the Crown Princess, her sister, the Princess Alice, once wrote, "There is a reflection of papa's great mind in her," while she said of that father's great thoughts and aims, " They can leave no one idle who knew of them."

While I have been gathering such small harvest of facts as may serve to illustrate these two royal lives, it has been above all things interesting to discover how *far-reaching* are those thoughts and aims of the Prince Consort to which his daughter alludes.—Of him our great poet has said very nobly—

> " He seems indeed mine own ideal knight,
> Who reverenced his conscience as his king,
> Whose glory was redressing human wrong.
> . . . We see him as he moved,
> How modest, kindly, all-accomplished, wise ;
> Wearing the white flower of a blameless life
> Before a thousand peering littlenesses,
> In that fierce light which beats upon a throne.
> . . . A Prince indeed
> Above all titles, and a household word
> Hereafter through all time, Albert the Good."

"Rex et Regina, right doers, those who direct and teach, as well as feed and clothe."—So writes Professor Ruskin of the kingly function.—May we not think of the two distinguished personages whose lives we are about to follow as likely to fulfil this definition of true kingship?

H.R.I.H. THE CROWN PRINCE OF GERMANY.

II.

BOYHOOD OF PRINCE FREDERICK WILLIAM.
[1831-1850.]

> "*This little one shall make it holiday.*"
> KING HENRY VIII.
> "*A noble boy, who would not do thee right?*"
> KING JOHN.

ON the 18th of October, 1831—the anniversary of the battle of Leipzig—"The blue eyes of 'Our Fritz' first opened to the sunshine of a bright autumn morning," says Frau Polko, weaving her pretty garland of prose and verse for the German people on the twenty-fifth wedding-day of their Imperial Prince and Princess. A month later this "promising offshoot from an ancient stem" received the names of Frederick William Nicholas Charles from the hands of Bishop Eylert, his grandfather's faithful old friend.—"Hear the little general: how well he gives the word of command!" said the people, when the sturdy babe cried lustily, wrapped in a robe enwoven with threads of Schleswig gold, and destined to be the christening garment henceforth of all German Imperial infants.

King Frederick William the Third was still reigning when his grandson, the only son of his second son, was born. His eldest son's marriage had proved childless, so this boy stood in the direct line of succession to the Prussian throne. The old king had lived through evil times. He had seen his native land ravaged by the armies of the conqueror—his territories parcelled out to the minions of Napoleon. His beautiful and talented wife, that Queen Louise whose memory is still revered in the Fatherland, died in 1810, broken-hearted to see her beloved country ground beneath the iron heel of the French Emperor. Once she had thrown herself at Napoleon's feet, beseeching him to spare the poor inhabitants of Magdeburg. His answer was to establish himself, when he marched on to Berlin, in the Queen's private rooms at Charlottenburg.—"But he did not sleep *in here*," said the nice little custodian who showed us those pretty, faded rooms, as she held back the curtains of the alcove where stands the Queen's own bed. "No! he carried his camp-bed with him wherever he went."—A faint fragrance of rose leaves still hangs about those old-fashioned rooms, with their soft Indian chintz hangings and their pale ribbons, which the Emperor William preserves in fond memory of his mother. The exquisite embroideries, wrought by her own hands during her last long illness, are covered carefully from sun and dust. "See the little *Stiefmütterchen* (wild heart's-ease) she worked herself!" whispered our guide, as she reverently uncovered a chair which had a group of tiny pansies thrown on its dim satin ground.

Down an alley in the gardens, bordered by cypress trees, stands the mausoleum where lie the still, white marble forms of the beautiful Queen and her husband. The sculptor Rauch has given to these figures — perhaps his masterpieces — a sublime expression of repose, of immortality. The garlands laid round them more than half a century ago are still green—green as is the memory of the good Queen's fortitude and devotion.

Her grandson, the little Prince Fritz, when he was carried out for the first time to take the air, was dressed in a tiny military cloak, with a soft little soldier's cap covering his tender flaxen head. When he could trot about, and gladden the fading eyes of his fond grandfather by frolicking round his knees, the little "Princekin" wore a recruit's uniform, and in that quaint garb he stood sobbing, when he was nine years old, by his kind old grandfather's deathbed. He had seen the first stone of the monument to Frederick the Great placed beneath the linden trees opposite the royal palaces in Berlin.

His only sister, the Princess Louise, named after her grandmother, was born in 1838.

Before he had completed his ninth year, our little Prince's military education began. His birthday gift to his father, in 1840, was a neatly written report of the guard at the Potsdam Gate. "It is one under-officer, one musician, eighteen grenadiers strong. Of watch and outposts nothing new to report."—A tender embrace and a hearty laugh were his recompence.

At ten, Prince Fritz was raised to the rank of sub-lieutenant, and solemnly invested by his uncle Frederick William IV. with the order of the Black Eagle. When the king, one Sunday, presented their new comrade to his brother officers after church parade he addressed him thus, "Dear Fritz!—Thou art still very little, yet learn to know these gentlemen; learn from them to do thy duty bravely; for he who would one day command must first of all learn to obey."

The new officer was very regular in his drill. One day it was raining in torrents when he was on parade before the palace. A servant ran out with an umbrella, and tried to hold it over the boy, but he cried out indignantly, "Hast thou ever seen a Prussian helmet under a *thing like that?*" and the poor man was forced to retreat with his umbrella, quite abashed.

But it would be wrong to suppose that the

education of this gracious and noble boy was exclusively of a military character. His mother, a Weimar princess, a disciple of Goethe, a friend of the Humboldts, "brought from the home of the Muses to the city of the great Frederick that element of universal culture which tempers the sterner virtues of the Hohenzollern race so well.

"The Emperor William is of the old heroic type, a true successor of Charlemagne, while those who converse with his son will find much of the cosmic, emotional spirit of Goethe in him. He judges of things by the standard of their truth, their goodness, their beauty. He may constantly be found removing obstacles to the welfare of the people with a gentle hand. He grasps the large, intelligent aspect of every question."

The Princess Augusta took anxious care to choose, from among the many able professors of the day, those instructors who might be most likely to awaken her son's artistic tastes, as well as to give him a solid grounding in all the branches of a good classical and modern education. In the year 1844 Dr. Ernest Curtius had attracted her attention by a lecture on the Acropolis of Athens, delivered in Berlin. "Imbued with an exquisite sense of the beautiful, Curtius treats of the fine arts, of history and mythology—even of grammar — with a fascinating eloquence." Dr. Curtius became tutor to Prince Frederick William when he was thirteen, superintending henceforth the lessons of the different masters employed to teach special subjects. While modern languages, music and drawing, dancing and horsemanship, were carefully attended to, the Prince also learnt two handicrafts, according to the tradition of the Hohenzollern race.—" Thus shall it be known that labour shames not the highest in the land; but rather that a practical knowledge of hand-work is one of the surest pillars on which our State rests," they say. So the heir to the throne might have been found in those days planing and sawing happily with the court carpenter, and binding books with the court bookbinder.

"Simple and manly was his bringing up; simple and modest did he remain in the days of his greatest military renown.[1] The best blessing of his childhood was the love of his parents, whose pride and joy he was. Those good seeds which nature had implanted in him were cherished, and mind and body were allowed to develop naturally and healthily."

His boyhood was chiefly spent at Babelsberg, near Potsdam. Here it was possible to enjoy a

[1] "Schlicht und einfach ist er bis zur Sonnenhöhe seines Ruhmes geblieben."

free, unconstrained country life, and to become, so to speak, personally acquainted with each of its beautiful trees and shrubs. Vacation rambles on foot, in many districts of Germany, began to be enjoyed so early as in 1841, when the Prince was only ten years old. In this pleasant fashion the Hartz district, the Thuringian Forest, the Franconian, and the Saxon Switzerland, were each in turn explored; while the principal seaport towns were frequently visited during the winter holidays.

When the Royal Family resided in Berlin, "our Fritz," and "our Louise," as they were sometimes called by the people, used to mix freely with the children around them.—"The goodies at Fuchs's never tasted so sweet to the little Berliners, the pantomime was never so much appreciated, as when the young Prince brought his little sister to share in these childish delights."

The Prince attained his majority with his eighteenth year. The day was spent at Babelsberg, where deputations were received from the civil and military services, and from the municipality; addresses of congratulation were presented, and the Prince was reminded that October 18th must always be a day of twofold rejoicing to the German people. They rejoiced in retrospect over a splendid national victory, and they rejoiced in prospect in the hopes which his career was likely to fulfil.

On November 7, 1849, Prince Frederick William entered the University of Bonn, and took up his residence there, with Dr. Curtius, and his military attachés, in the palace of the former Kurfürsts. Since the year 1837, when the two Princes of Saxe-Coburg-Gotha had graduated at the Rhenish College, it had been a favourite resort of the German royal princes. In 1849 political disturbances were rife throughout the whole of the Fatherland, and at first the Prussian Prince may have been regarded with some prejudice.—" By no artifice of kingcraft, beyond that of having an honest, kindly word for every one, and *remembering* every one, Prince Frederick William had soon however overcome all hostile feeling. He pursued his studies at Bonn with that zest which distinguishes him in all that he sets his mind to accomplish."

One March day in 1850, a gaily-decked steamer was seen coming swiftly up the Rhine. As it approached Bonn, it stopped to take a young student on board, for this boat was conveying the Prince and Princess of Prussia to the old palace at Coblentz, where they were about to take up their residence for some years, the Prince being at that period Military Commandant of the Rhenish provinces, Westphalia, and the army of occupation in Baden.

As they approached Coblentz—"Where the glad waters of the Moselle fling themselves into the stately Rhine-flood, the river becomes enchantingly pretty. It is here girdled about with hills, and each crag has its legendary castle; the beetling precipices of Ehrenbreitstein rise from the green waters, crowned with that fortress which looks across to the old town with its historical gates and its royal palace. When the steamer neared the landing-stage at Coblentz, a tall, slender youth might have been seen standing on the deck, his arm thrown protectingly round a little girl of eleven. She was clasping a great doll tenderly in her arms, glancing from its friendly face to the cheering crowds waiting to bid the royal party welcome."

The life at the old palace during the years which followed has been described as quite idyllic —*idyllisch*—a word of a finer flavour than our equivalent for it, according to Professor Max Müller.—The Princess of Prussia was not only a beautiful and brilliant woman, but she had early learnt to value the society of clever men, and often collected round her tea-table the first minds of the day, so as to create a second Weimar by the Rhine. Bonn was close at hand, and when young people were invited to enjoy the dance and song, to join in dramatic performances, with all that happy unconstraint so rarely to be enjoyed at court, her son often came to enliven the circle and make it gay.

A hundred little anecdotes were told of the brother and sister in those merry days—of how they visited the neighbouring fairs, and came away after spending their modest pocket money on gifts for father or mother—of how they were to be seen arm in arm, the little pug dog trotting beside them —that favourite dog, which had its *parure* also, when the Princess was betrothed, when almost a child, to the Prince Regent of Baden.—The Princess Augusta exercised her taste in laying out the pretty "Anlagen," those long, green arcades by the river's brink, for which the people of Coblentz owe her so much gratitude.—When we saw these arcades this summer (1886), they looked more charming than ever, while the garden in front of the Castle, open to every one, was brilliant with variegated leaves and fine colouring.

The young Prince made pleasant friendships in his trips up and down the broad river, and his visits to many neighbouring towns. Men of all shades of religious and political opinions were interesting to him; he conversed with equal pleasure with Cardinal von Geissel, the accomplished ultramontane prelate of Cologne, and with von Möller, the statesman and philosopher. The Prince accompanied his father to Carlsruhe when Prince Anthony of Hohenzollern Sigmaringen made his famous speech on yielding up the suzerainty of his kingdom to the Prussian Crown, on the 30th of April, 1850.

"If," said the Prince of Sigmaringen on that memorable occasion, "the unification of all the German States can be effected, the desire of every true patriot will be fulfilled. No sacrifice would be too great to make for so great a consummation as this. I myself am now laying the greatest gift that man can bestow on the altar of the Fatherland. May my people be happy under their new and glorious sovereign!"

The Grand Duke of Baden had previously given in his adhesion to the Prussian Crown.

In May, 1850, Princess Charlotte of Prussia[1] was married to the Duke of Saxe-Meiningen. When the Crown Prince was present in Berlin at this wedding, he could scarcely foresee that his own daughter would marry the son of this favourite cousin, a quarter of a century later. During the autumn he stayed with these relatives at their villa by the shores of the Lake of Como. The Prince then made a further tour in Switzerland, the Tyrol, and France, before returning to Bonn for the autumn session.

[1] Cousin of Prince Frederick William.

A longer and more important journey was in prospect for him. The first great International Exhibition, which was occupying every one's thoughts in the spring of 1851, was about to open in London, and an invitation to be present at its inaugural ceremony had been sent by our Queen to the Prussian royal family.

On April 27th Prince Frederick William set foot on English soil for the first time, little dreaming of those ties which were one day to bind him so closely to our nation, and to our Sovereign.

III.

PRINCE FREDERICK WILLIAM VISITS ENGLAND.
[1851-1855.]

> *"This bud of love, by Summer's ripening breath,*
> *May prove a beauteous flower when next we meet."*
> ROMEO AND JULIET.

PRINCE ALBERT'S great scheme of a "Peace Congress," which might bring all the nations of the earth together for their mutual benefit, had reached its brilliant completion. The peoples of the East and of the West were gathered beneath those flashing, crystal domes which had risen, "like a bow in the cloud," from the green turf in Hyde Park, and were waiting to greet the author of this splendid world's show, when Prince Frederick William saw London one bright May morning in the year 1851 in its most festive mood.

We read the Queen's touching description of that day, so long gone by, with interest and emotion this year, when—"taking her courage in both hands"—she has met her people once more on a similar occasion; but under such changed conditions. Those who were present last May, when the Queen proclaimed the opening of the Colonial Exhibition in her own clear, unfaltering tones, came away to speak softly of the great tears which were on her cheek as she stood once more in the presence of a vast expectant multitude. They said, too, how close at her mother's side had been the Crown Princess, her eldest child, who could share in every recollection of 1851, and who was shaken by pangs of memory as keen as those which moved our high-hearted Sovereign.

The Queen's diary, quoted by Sir Theodore Martin, recorded in May, 1851, that the "Sight was magical, so vast, so glorious, so touching; one felt—many did whom I have spoken to—filled with devotion, more so than at any service I have ever heard. The tremendous cheers, the joy expressed by every face, the immensity of the building, with its flowers, palms, statues, fountains; my beloved husband, the author of this Peace Festival, which unites the industries of all the nations of the earth. . . . . All this was moving indeed; it was a day to live for ever. I felt so grateful to the great God who seemed to pervade it all, and bless it all."

Thackeray's "May Day Ode" in commemoration of that great spectacle ends with these lines:

" . . . Behold her in her royal place,
A gentle lady, and the hand,
That sways the sceptre of this land,
    How frail and weak !

Soft is the voice, and fair the face ;
She breathes 'Amen' to prayer and hymn ;
No wonder that her eyes are dim,
    And pale her cheek.

Swell, organ, swell your triumph blast,
March, Queen and royal pageant, march,
By splendid aisle and springing arch,
    Of this fair hall ;

And see ! above the fabric vast,
God's boundless heaven is bending, blue,
God's peaceful sunlight beaming through ;
    It shines o'er all ! "

It shone on the young head of Victoria, Princess Royal of Great Britain and Ireland, as she clung to the hand of her father, her clear eyes fixed on the moving spectacle before her. It shone also on the fair locks of a tall, noble-looking youth, standing near her—a youth somewhat resembling the Scandinavian heroes who once landed on our northern coasts, of a "most pleasant countenance," gentle and strong.

"Under such exciting circumstances did 'our Fritz' first behold the future companion of his life, the dear mother of his children, . . . that 'fair rose of England,' then only in its tender bud, but one day to take root and blossom in German soil. The future Crown Princess of Germany was as yet only ten years old, but might not his prophetic soul even then have been able to discern the flower in the bud ? "

Prince Frederick William paid a long visit to England at this time. He was always more and more impressed with the spectacle of the loyalty of a free people. He admired our constitutional institutions and government. He was struck with wonder and delight to see the ceaseless industry of the Prince Consort. Above all things, however, was he attracted by the—" Perfect domestic happiness which he found pervading the heart, and core, and focus of the greatest Empire in the world."

Yet the young German Prince was loyal to his own boyish home and haunts, even when most impressed by the historical monuments of England. One day he had been expressing that admiration for our ancient Windsor Castle which most foreigners feel so strongly. Presently he turned to a friend who was standing near and said—" But you should see Babelsberg, it is so much prettier ! "—Dr. von Bunsen, who relates this speech, adds, " Surely a youth cannot be far wrong who prefers his own little snuggery to the splendours of a foreign palace." From the same source we hear that, after gazing fixedly one day at an Italian picture at Windsor, the Prince turned to his companion and said—" Is not that Saint of Titian's very like the Princess Royal?"—Dr. von Bunsen then proceeds to relate how his father, then *chargé d'affaires* at the English Court, may have been the first to suggest the fitness of an alliance with England, in a manner which reminds one of the *esprit* of a former century. During a visit to London, to see her aged relative, the Queen Dowager, undertaken in 1852, by the Prince's mother, now Empress of Germany, the Prussian envoy was waiting for an interview in an anteroom filled with splendid engravings sent by print-sellers for the inspection of the Princess. He had been looking at the famous picture of Waterloo, with the farmhouse of " La Belle Alliance," from which the Belgians have named the battle, in the foreground. Observing several portraits of the Princess Royal and of Prince Frederick William lying about the room, he hastily placed one of each over the large engraving of the battle as he quitted the table to bow to her Royal Highness.—The Princess saw two smiling young faces looking at her as she approached the table, and underneath them these words: " La Belle Alliance."—" A rapid glance was exchanged, but not a word spoken "—adds Dr. von Bunsen.

Prince Frederick William returned to Berlin in time to command a company of the old palace guard when Rauch's equestrian statue of Frederick the Great was unveiled, on the 31st of May, 1851. When the covering fell, and the splendid bronze figure stood revealed, the King embraced the sculptor before the eyes of innumerable spectators.

The royal student was again at Bonn when the college term opened in October. Here he pursued his studies with unabated interest for two more sessions, before quitting the university after the Easter session of 1852.

When he left Bonn the Prince was gazetted to a captaincy in the first foot-guards. He was zealous in his regimental duties, sparing himself no work, and claiming no exemption from the routine pursued by his brother officers. In Germany, the regimental duties of officers are very different from such duties in England.

I once asked a lieutenant in the *Garde Reiter*, the first German cavalry regiment, "What are you teaching your men at present?" "Oh! history and geography in our afternoon class," replied the young baron. His brother had been gazetted a few weeks before to the same regiment. One evening this pretty boy was trying vainly to keep awake. "You see," he said, in apology, "we get up at four o'clock every morning, and for six weeks after we join we have to groom our own horses, also." These young officers belong to one of the oldest Saxon families, and have, each in turn, served as pages to the king while passing through the "Caditten Haus" in Dresden.

But not only did the Prince instruct his men; he knew each man—his circumstances, his affairs—individually. To celebrate his twenty-first birthday he gave them a fête, when he came amongst them, like a comrade, to join in the merriment, and encourage the song and dance.

During the summer of 1852, the Empress of Russia visited Berlin on her homeward journey from the German baths. It was hinted that some jealousy might possibly be felt in Russian circles, from the fact of the young Prince's first journey beyond the bounds of Germany having been to England, and he now accompanied his aunt to St. Petersburg.

"Russia, under the Czar Nicholas, presented a spectacle little pleasing to our young Prince, for a despotic monarch was then ruling over a nation debased by slavery. Under a brilliant surface a rotten core was hidden, and this contrasted badly with the Prince's observations during his visit to the "sea-girt Isle."

It was during this year that Colonel von Moltke came for the first time into personal relations with Prince Frederick William. A warm friendship then grew up between the great mathematician and his pupil, which years were to develop more fully. Helmuth von Moltke—*heller Muth*, bright courage —how singularly appropriate is the name of this great statesman!—" The noble family of Moltke comes of old time from the island of Möen, where you may find its monumental brasses in the older churches to this day. Three moorhens on a shield argent are surmounted there by a helm from which wave seven peacock's feathers. In the crusading days the peacock was a sacred bird, no emblem of pride, but a mirror of eternity. An old Christian legend tells that, on the day of its creation, the smile of the Eternal fell upon this creature as it passed, pranking itself in all its beauty, and that its fan-like tail caught and reflected the Divine glance. Seven feathers did the race of Moltke bear on their crest, for seven is the knightly number. Those seven eyes behold the struggles in the good knight's breast between the seven deadly sins and the virtues. . . . *Candide et caute* —the motto of this ancient family—how well it describes their great descendant !—Candid and cautious."

Reader, can you forgive this digression? The

little peacock legend seemed too pretty to remain only a German possession.

The climate of Berlin is trying when dry, biting winds prevail, as they do at certain seasons of the year, and in the spring of 1853 Prince Frederick William was seized with an attack of acute inflammation of the lungs. When able to travel, he was sent to Ems for milder air, and it was afterwards thought desirable that he should seek a more southern climate. He resided at Vevey, by the beautiful shores of the lake of Geneva, during the autumn of 1853, when he became an ardent admirer of mountain scenery while exploring the valleys of Switzerland. In November he was again in Berlin, preparing for a more lengthened visit to the south. He was then enrolled as a Freemason. The Liberal party rejoiced to hear of this step, which they regarded as a protest against both religious intolerance and political persecution. No Prussian monarch, with the exception of Frederick the Great, had ever before belonged to the ancient brotherhood; although the Prince of Prussia was a Freemason. When presenting his son for initiation into the mysteries of the craft, the Prince exhorted him to become—" A strenuous supporter of this Order, for not only wilt thou thereby benefit thyself, but thou wilt have the consciousness that thou art also labouring to promote what is excellent in others by this means."

In December the young Prince set forth for Rome, with several men distinguished in letters and in art in his suite. The party took up their quarters in the house once occupied by Count Harry von Arnim and were soon in full enjoyment of all the artistic and social delights of the Eternal City.

Pio Nono received the young Hohenzollern Prince with distinguished courtesy, throwing open to him the private collections at the Vatican, and offering every facility for his greater enjoyment of the wonders of Rome. A splendid fête was given in his honour, when the sculpture galleries of the Pope's palace were illuminated by "wind torches." The effect of this magic light, as it flickered upon statues and on guests alike, has been described as strange and weird.—The marble forms seemed actually to breathe and move, the spectators to be transformed to stone.

A personal regard and affection grew up, at this time, between these two men of such different characters and aims, which survived through all the embittered political strife of after years. The benevolent and dignified spiritual sovereign delighted in this manly, straightforward representative of a great Protestant dynasty, who possessed such wide sympathies, and so eager an appreciation of the beauties of art and of nature.

The Eternal City was indeed a source of endless

delight to the Prince. He explored its ancient monuments with ever-increasing zest and wonder; he visited the studios of artists of every nationality; he attended the weekly meetings of the Archæological Society; he entered freely into the brilliant social life of Rome, which included in its circles many of his distinguished compatriots. One of the houses most frequently visited by the Prince was that of Frei-Frau von Bülow, the accomplished daughter of William von Humboldt. The old Italian nobility, the Dorias, the Borgheses, the Colonnas, and other great historical families who were then living in Rome, threw open their doors to the northern Prince with equal cordiality.

All too soon the delightful days fled away, and it was with reluctance that the Prince left Rome for the southern Italian provinces in March. He then visited Pompeii and Herculaneum, Naples and Sorrento, before proceeding to see the historical cities of Piedmont and Lombardy. In these, then subject lands of Northern Italy, he is said to have been painfully impressed with the contrast, everywhere visible, between the beauty and abundance of nature, and the down-trodden, poverty-stricken aspect of the inhabitants. When visiting the kingdom of Sardinia, however, the Prince saw that great man who was one day to loosen the chains of these poor people, and who was then living under the strong protecting arm of King Victor Emanuel. When he met the young Hohenzollern Prince, Cavour did not foresee how much reason Italy might have for gratitude to the conqueror of Königgrätz in the far-off future. The historian, who describes that battle, has said that, "Austria lost no German territory by that great defeat, but Italy set her foot once more on the shores of the Adriatic."

The Prince and Princess of Prussia celebrated their silver wedding in the early summer of 1854. Their son returned from Italy to join in the public rejoicings which then took place in Berlin, and soon afterwards resumed his military duties with renewed ardour. During the autumn manœuvres of this year, the Prince was to be seen, on the hottest and dustiest days, marching at the head of his troops. He lived the same camp life as the private soldier, shared the fatigues of his men, and messed often with the citizens belonging to the militia.

During the winter months he studied in the Military Academy under Colonel von Unruh. This gentleman tells an anecdote which shows the eager interest taken by the Princess Augusta in all that concerned the welfare of her son. Once the Colonel was summoned to an audience by this anxious mother, who wished to impress upon him the importance of strict discipline, and of the performance of every duty by her son.—"All at once," he relates, "the door opened and the Prince of Prussia came in. 'Ah! So our new tutor has come to *la chère maman* for orders?' he said, laughingly, as he shook hands with me.—' Now, he is not going to receive *one* from me.—My dear,' added the Prince in a low voice, ' this young fellow is a pupil of my own, I taught him, and now he is going to teach our boy.'"

Early in the year 1855 Prince Frederick William set forth, accompanied by General von Moltke, on a prolonged tour of the Prussian province. Many old historical localities were visited which recalled the memories of the Kurfürsts of Brandenburg, of the Teutonic knights, of many brave deeds and important events. Everywhere the heir to the throne was received with rejoicings, and warmly welcomed. Everywhere he made himself acquainted with the circumstances, the hopes and wishes of the citizens in the chief Prussian towns through which he passed. The last halt was made at Dantzig. This important old town, with its " Noble architecture, which in itself speaks for the self-respecting character of its inhabitants," interested the Prince in a peculiar manner. One evening a fire had broken out, and he was one of the first to reach the scene of the conflagration. The report of his exertions in extinguishing the flames reached a little country village where the

Prince was assisting at a rustic fête, on the following day, when it added to the enthusiasm of his reception by the country folk.

As the autumn of 1855 approached, the Prince's thoughts turned in a new direction, and a journey was planned, fraught with great results to Germany as well as to Germany's future Emperor.

IV.

BETROTHAL OF PRINCE FREDERICK WILLIAM.

[1855-1858.]

> "*Fair Princess,
> Wilt thou vouchsafe to teach a soldier terms
> Such as may enter at a lady's ear
> And plead his love-suit to her gentle heart?*"
> KING HENRY V.

IN the pleasant month of September, 1855, Prince Frederick William had nearly completed his twenty-fourth year.—" The youth had become a man, a man too who often felt himself alone in the midst of all his active pursuits and public duties, and who longed for that domestic happiness which can only be found in the companionship of a beloved and sympathetic wife." — We can scarcely wonder if the Prince's thoughts turned frequently to England, and to the perfect domestic life he had been privileged to witness when he visited her royal palace four years before; nor would it be strange if the image of that charming young girl, who even then seemed to him to resemble Titian's Saint, now presented itself in bright colours to his memory and imagination.

One bright autumnal evening, when all the Scotch hill-sides were wrapped in a mantle of purple heather, a young knight came to the gates of an enchanted castle set far away amongst the rugged mountains of the north.—The portals opened to him, and there he found the fairy princess of his dreams—found her "holy, fair, and wise," as his imagination had pictured her; but—still so young! How could he venture to disturb the "maiden meditation" of one who had scarcely completed her fifteenth year? Yet happily our Princess Royal was mature in mind and character beyond her years. From her earliest childhood she had lived in close companionship with her father, and that companionship was in itself a rare education.

"A breath of poetry hangs round those days, so filled with the purest happiness of the young Prince's wooing," says the German biographer, and indeed the brief record of that wooing, as we find it in the "Life of the Prince Consort," reads more like some pastoral tale, some page of old romance, than the statement of a great fact in modern history. The Queen and Prince had at first given their guest to understand that their child was as yet too young to be disturbed by any thoughts of marriage; yet after many days of suspense, there came one propitious afternoon when Prince Frederick William found himself wandering over the heath-clad hills with the young Princess. Suddenly he espied a spray of white heather—that emblem of good luck—He gathered it quickly, he presented it to the Princess; it gave him courage to speak of his hopes—*On devine ceux qui nous aiment*—and with this pure badge the bride was won!

When Prince Frederick William's visit had ended, the Prince Consort, always mindful of that faithful friend at Coburg, who entertained so especial a regard and admiration for his "wonderfully wise *Prinzesschen*," wrote thus to Baron Stockmar:—"The young people are ardently in love with one another. . . . The purity, innocence, and unselfishness of the young man are touching. At parting, abundance of tears were shed. . . . My feeling was rather one of cheerful satisfaction, and gratitude to God for bringing across our path so much that is noble and good. . . . We are quite unprepared for any public declaration of the betrothal at present. . . . The secret must be kept *tant bien que mal*. . . . The actual marriage cannot be thought of till the seventeenth birthday is past."

Yet the secret was already an open one when *The Times*, unable to forecast what Germany was one day to owe to the Hohenzollern race, and guided by the unpopularity in England of the then existing Prussian government, put forth a violent article, which wound up with the prediction that our Princess might one day come back to us a fugitive, banished from the land of her adoption! "The English in their self-reliance are prejudiced against all foreigners," is the comment of Herr Hengst on this strangely ignorant attack on the Prussian nation and dynasty. "Very different," he adds, "was the feeling in Germany with regard to the English marriage." The small but powerful faction then at the helm of our vessel of state, might perhaps regard British influence with suspicion, taking their cue, as they did, from Russia, but the people, the nation, hailed the news of the English alliance with unbounded satisfaction. No choice could have roused the sympathy of his people more warmly; they rejoiced to hear that their young Prince, of whom they knew so much that was delightful, and foresaw so much that was excellent, should have chosen a daughter of "free England" for his bride. Prince Frederick William had set himself in accord with the wishes of his people, and the feeling of contentment which the nation now experienced strengthened and sanctified anew the bond between the heir to the throne and the German nation.

"At the same time—on the very same day on which our young Prince told his love to the Princess Royal in the distant Scottish Highlands—his sister and the Prince Regent Frederick of Baden plighted their troth at Coblentz. The Princess of Prussia had the rare happiness of celebrating the betrothal of both her children on her own birthday."

Stimulated, as it may well be supposed, by his recent intercourse with Prince Albert, Prince Frederick William, after his return home, applied his mind to affairs of state during the winter of 1855-6—"to the infinite satisfaction of the people, who knew that what he set himself to do would be accomplished thoroughly, and with an unprejudiced mind and judgment." The more his horizon widened in relation to the conduct of state affairs, the greater was his aversion to the system of government then prevailing in Prussia. The Manteuffel ministry was at that period resorting to many unconstitutional devices in order to ensure the return of its own nominees in the pending elections; and so strongly did the young Prince feel in regard to these proceedings, that—to use his biographer's phrase—"he shook out his heart," soon after his return from England, in writing to his future father-in-law on this subject. Prince Albert's important letter in reply is given *in extenso* in Herr Hengst's book. Its concluding sentence runs thus: "I would record my solemn protest against such doings, from no desire for popularity, but solely in defence of the just rights of my fellow-citizens, my Fatherland. By doing so you may sustain the people in hope, and hope is the best nurse of patience." In a later letter, Prince Albert said, in allusion to his future son-in-law's immediate studies, "You tell, in your letter to Victoria the third,[1] of new studies and occupations in ministerial departments; I fear, when you have had experience for some time of these departments, you will realize the truth of Axel Oxenstierna's saying, 'My son, thou wilt wonder to find with how little wisdom the world is governed.'"

In May, 1856, the Prince had the happiness of spending some time with his promised bride. England was then celebrating the proclamation of peace by splendid illuminations and fêtes. The London season was at its height, and many delightful festivities offered themselves to the betrothed couple during this merry month. On a bright May day, the University of Oxford bestowed the degree of LL.D. on Prince Frederick William, in conjunction with his future brother-in-law, the Prince Regent of Baden. A German paper describes the Oxford commemoration as

[1] The Duchess of Kent was also named Victoria.

"The memorial festival in honour of the founders of the university—a celebration which unites the grave and the gay aspects of life. Sermons and lectures alternate with processions of boats on the river, flower-shows and concerts. . . . . The Earl of Derby, the chancellor of the university, took his seat at eleven o'clock in the (so-called) theatre, Prince Albert at his right hand, the two young German Princes at his left. . . . Degrees were also bestowed on Count Bernstorff, Prussian ambassador, Lord Clarendon, Lord Elgin, Sir Edmund Lyons, and the German traveller, Dr. Barth. . . . Haydn's Creation was performed afterwards; Mdme. Jenny Lind-Goldschmidt and Mdme. Viardot Garcia taking part in it."

The more closely the young Hohenzollern Prince became acquainted with English life and English institutions, the more did he value the social and political principles on which England's greatness rests. Soon, too, English hearts began to turn to this young man, as the charm of his mind and character, and of his straightforward, kindly manner, was felt more widely. He saw the great races at Epsom and Ascot; he visited the arsenal at Woolwich, the camp at Aldershot, as well as the University of Cambridge, on the occasion of his present visit. On the eve of his departure from London, an alarming accident befell the Princess Royal. It was thus described in a letter written by the Prince Consort, with his never-failing consideration for others, to reassure Baron Stockmar as to the safety of the Princess:

"June 25th, 1856.

"I write to tell you of an accident which might have proved very disastrous, but which, thank God, has passed off happily. I should not like you to get your first news of it from the papers. Vicky was sealing a letter at the table when, all at once, she was in flames, her sleeve having caught fire at the candle. Miss Hillyard was luckily sitting at the same table; Mrs. Anderson was giving Alice a music-lesson in the room. They sprang at once to her assistance, and extinguished the flames with the hearth-rug. Nevertheless, the right arm is severely burnt from below the elbow to the shoulder. Sir Benjamin Brodie has examined the wound with his microscope, and is satisfied that, except on a small spot, the lower skin is uninjured, and that no permanent disabling of the arm is to be dreaded. The poor child showed very great self-possession and presence of mind at the time, and great courage under the pain. . . . Naturally we were very much alarmed, and the poor bridegroom [1] quite upset."

[1] A betrothed couple are called bride and bridegroom before marriage in Germany.

On his return home an important event called for the presence of Prince Frederick William in Russia. The Czar Alexander had announced that his coronation was about to take place in Moscow; the European sovereigns were sending their representatives to be present at the splendid ceremonial, and the Prussian King, so closely allied to Russia, had decided that his future heir should be present, to do honour to the great occasion. On the Prince's brilliant staff were Generals von Moltke and Heinitz, Prince William Radziwill and his son, General Freiherr von Schreckenstein, Prince Leopold of Hohenzollern, and many other notable persons. The Prince's aunt, the Empress-mother of Russia, came from Wildbad, where she had been residing for the benefit of her enfeebled health, to Sans Souci. From thence she proceeded, under escort of her nephew, to Russia, "To give her maternal blessing to her son at his coronation, as is the beautiful old custom in that land."

The foregoing is taken from General von Moltke's letters from Russia, quoted by Herr Hengst as giving vivid descriptions of the splendid ceremonial which he then witnessed at Moscow, as well as strange accounts of the journey and of the immense number of horses utilized by the Prussian party in its accomplishment. The following passage may give some idea of the curious scene presented by the ancient Russian capital during the week of the coronation solemnities.

"*Friday.*—The whole diplomatic corps came to pay their respects to-day to the Prince (Frederick William). Count Morny, Prince Esterhazy, Lord Granville, Prince de Ligne, all in gala uniforms and state carriages. . . . With his own peculiar ease, and assisted by his prodigious memory for persons and events, the Prince had something suitable to say to each.

"*Saturday.*—The Prince received to-day fifty to sixty different potentates from Mongolia, Kurdistan, Tartary, Mingrelia, the Caucasus, Circassia, Dagestan, etc. All wore their national costumes, and were resplendent in jewels, cloth of gold, and splendid arms."

The coronation presented a picture full of pomp and poetry—

"The Emperor looked grave, but kindly; he seemed to feel the full significance of the solemn ceremony, not because of its earthly pomp, but in spite of it. It would be hard to conceive of anything more fairy-like than that old city, spread out beneath the beams of the sun, and filled with everything that is splendid and exalted from far and near. Between its oldest monuments and most sacred shrines that long train wound along, bearing the treasures of the church, the weapons of the warrior, the regalia of the Crown, beneath the blue vault of heaven, as it came on to greet the new Emperor."

On the 20th of September the marriage of the Princess Louise of Prussia with the Prince Regent of Baden was solemnized in Berlin. In order to give English readers a glimpse of this lady's character, I have translated a portion of a letter, written by her in the second year of her marriage, to the venerable Alexander von Humboldt. The original appears in Frau Polko's little book, already quoted in these pages.—" I recall with gratitude," writes the Grand Duchess of Baden, "the many occasions when I have ventured to exchange thoughts with you, the many proofs you have continually given me, from my childhood, of your kindly sympathy. It is my warmest wish to see you again now that I am a wife and a mother, to listen with redoubled interest and reverence to your words. . . . Since we last met, my life has become so much more beautiful, more precious, to me, my happiness is so much richer and deeper than before. . . . This dear child seems to have brought it to a height undreamt of till now. . . . If I could but show you the little creature, I know you would delight in it."

In after years the Grand Duchess of Baden became the close neighbour and friend of our Princess Alice, Grand Duchess of Hesse Darmstadt. She and her husband are that " good Fritz and Louise of Baden," always referred to with an expression of sympathy or of pleasure, in our Queen's diaries. They are good rulers, and beloved by their people of the Duchy, whose large, warm-brown cottages, with pretty gardens and well-tilled fields stretching out from them, strike the eye pleasantly on entering the Baden territories. Every one speaks with an affectionate pride of the Duke and Duchess in the clean, cheerful, old town of Constance, where you hear of their simple home life in their summer residence close by. Mainau has been described with a few graphic touches by Lady Verney, in her book on "Peasant Proprietors," together with the amiable royal family who give to it its charm.

Prince Frederick William commanded the 11th regiment of infantry which was garrisoned at Breslau during the autumn months of 1856. As November approached, however, he left the Silesian capital for Berlin, and in a few days found himself once more with the Princess Royal in London, when he was announced as coming, "To congratulate the Princess on her approaching birthday"—all that might, for the time, be said. The royal family was mourning the loss of the Queen's half-brother, the Prince of Leiningen, when the Prussian Prince arrived. A very tender affection had existed between the Princess Royal and her uncle, to which Prince Albert refers when he writes at this date—" Prince Fritz William is with us; his visit is a sad one. Still, as he looks forward to sharing many griefs as well as joys with Vicky, their sympathy in this sorrow is but one tie the more."

In December the young Prince returned *viâ* Paris, which he had not previously visited, to Breslau, to take up his residence there at the royal palace for the winter. Here he became the centre of a distinguished circle, and exercised hospitality to persons of every rank and shade of religious and political opinion. Though his military duties were engrossing, he often, during the winter months, attended the sittings of the provincial government, entering with never-failing interest into affairs connected with the local administration of the province.

Many excursions were made to the surrounding districts, when the Prince was able to see the industrial wealth of this portion of the eastern province, described by Fräulein Sohr as so " rich in mills and great manufactories."—" Here," she writes, " you are struck by the many proofs of beneficent care bestowed upon their workpeople by the large employers of labour. The great mills are invariably surrounded by colonies of neat little one-storied houses, each possessing its pretty garden and grass plat. The school, the church, the cottage hospital, stand close by, as does the house of 'the master.' From this, as from a focus, spread morality, order, peace, and prosperity. The 'mistress,' too, uses her influence to bring happiness and thrift to the whole community. You may say that such social conditions as these which prevail in my own Silesian home are exceptional, that they belong to the small *élite* of the commercial aristocracy, that the weaver's life is generally squalid—the lot of the miner sad and dangerous. Perhaps so. The moral influence of such communities as I indicate is, nevertheless, increasing, and the principles on which they exist are an important factor in modern life. . . . Those industrial occupations which create mutual duties and obligations of the highest kind, where generation after generation may have worked together, receiving and bestowing reciprocal benefits, are worthy of our highest respect."

The foregoing is the substance of a passage from Fräulein Sohr's book, too long for insertion *in extenso*. It is a fact known to all, that the future rulers of Germany hold in high estimation that "industrial aristocracy" which is of comparatively recent growth in the Fatherland. The Hohenzollerns have always fostered the manufactures of their country, and our English Princess loves to encourage every kind of industrial work which may tend to make the people of Germany independent and self-respecting. The Prince, it is said, won golden opinions during his long visit to the eastern provinces by his intelligent appreciation of every important question, and by the kindly sincerity of his interest in all who came into contact with him.

In the month of May, 1857, he was again in England. And now the royal engagement was publicly announced, when honours and distinctions were conferred upon the future husband of our Princess by the learned and municipal councils of many of our great towns. In presenting the Prussian Prince with the freedom of the City of London, the City Chamberlain made a speech which was reported in the English papers as concluding with these words—"Our native land, and Germany, is each giving its best treasure, to be knit together in a bond which will promote peace and goodwill over the whole earth."

The Queen's youngest child was born in April, 1857, and christened early in June, her eldest sister and future brother-in-law being sponsors to the little Princess Beatrice.

The first distribution of the Victoria Cross took place in Hyde Park on June 26th. The Queen then rode into the Park—"Mounted on her favourite roan, dressed in a scarlet jacket and black skirt, and accompanied by the Prince Consort, Prince Frederick William of Prussia, and a brilliant suite. Remaining on horseback, her Majesty pinned the cross, with her own hand, upon the breast of each man as he was brought up to her, and to each Prince Albert bowed with marked respect as he withdrew."—"A magnificent spectacle "—is his comment on this most striking occasion of the day.

On the 29th the royal party, including Prince Frederick William, left London for Manchester, to visit the "Exhibition of Art Treasures," which Prince Albert had been so largely instrumental in organizing.—"Everywhere were kind allusions to Fritz and Vicky," says the Queen's diary; the Mayor presented an address to the Prussian Prince, to which he made—"A very clear and able reply, which was received with much applause by all present."

During the autumn months Prince Frederick William was present at the military manœuvres at Reichenbach. In November he was again in England, when the Princess Royal celebrated her seventeenth birthday. When he then quitted her, it was to return for the last time alone to Berlin.

On the following 21st of January the Prince set forth on what is called in Germany the "Brautfahrt"—The journey to bring home his bride.

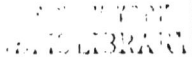

H.R.I.H. THE CROWN PRINCESS OF GERMANY.

V.

CHILDHOOD OF THE PRINCESS ROYAL.

[1840-1847.]

> "*This royal infant (heaven still move about her !)
> Though in her cradle yet, now promises
> . . . A thousand, thousand blessings,
> Which time shall bring to ripeness: she shall be
> A pattern to all Princes living with her
> And all that shall succeed.*"
>
> KING HENRY VIII.

JOY-BELLS were pealing, cannon booming, through all the length and breadth of England on the morning of the 21st of November, 1840, for the glad tidings had gone forth that a royal babe was born, and the people were rejoicing to know that their young Queen was safe, and that the succession to the throne was now assured.

The Times of the day describes the new-born babe as "a plump, healthy, and beautiful Princess," and relates, moreover, that within a few hours of her birth—verifying Baron Stockmar's dictum, that a man's education begins on the first day of his life—wrapped in flannels and placed upon a table in Buckingham Palace, she gave audience to certain lords of the Privy Council and other notabilities. *The Times* adds that the little Princess proved the soundness of her lungs by the loud tones in which she testified her disapproval of this unseemly intrusion on her privacy.

A Queen regnant must forego a mother's privilege, and entrust her child to the fostering care of a nurse. A Scotch lady had been chosen to fill this important office, and the royal infant grew apace under her care.—Just eighteen years later the people of Berlin were stirred to admiration to know that a young mother was herself nursing her first-born son in the royal palace in their midst.[1]

This future mother of Emperors was christened on the anniversary of the Queen's wedding-day, receiving the names of Victoria Adelaide Mary Louisa.—" How the little lady looked about her," said Lord Melbourne to the Queen afterwards, " as if quite conscious that all the stir was about herself.—This is the time when character is shown."

" Your little great-grandchild behaved with great

[1] Letters from an aunt of the writer's, then living in Berlin, say, " Everybody is charmed to hear that our Princess is nursing her baby herself."

propriety, and like a Christian," wrote Prince Albert to the Dowager-Duchess of Saxe-Gotha a few days later, " she was awake, but did not cry at all; she crowed with immense satisfaction and delight at the lights and the brilliant uniforms, for already she is very intelligent and observing."

When their little daughter was born the Queen and Prince Consort were but just twenty-one.[1] A week before the Princess Royal celebrated her first birthday a little brother had come to her. The Queen's diary, as quoted in the " Life of the Prince Consort," gives, in a few simple words, a charming picture of her year-old daughter on the 21st of November, 1841. The Queen says—" Albert brought in dearest little Pussy, in such a smart white merino dress trimmed with blue, which mamma had given her, and a pretty cap, and placed her on the bed, seating himself beside her. She was very dear and good. As my precious, invaluable Albert sat there, our little love between us, I felt quite moved with happiness and gratitude to God." At Rheinhardtsbrunn, in the Thuringian Forest, there is a sweet little crayon drawing by the Queen of her baby daughter, hanging on a bedroom wall in a modest frame. The round, rosy creature, in a quaint little cap, smiles in the friendliest fashion on the passing stranger.

[1] The Queen and Prince were born in 1819, within three months of each other.

Two more years have gone swiftly by, and the Princess is growing, to quote from the Queen's maternal record, "quite a little personage," who speaks French and English with "great fluency, and choice of phrases . . . Pussette . . . learns a verse of Lamartine by heart, which ends with '*le tableau se déroule à mes pieds.*' To show how well she understands this difficult line, I must tell you"—the Queen is writing to her uncle, the king of the Belgians—"the following *bon-mot*. When she was riding on her pony and looking at the cows and sheep, she turned to her governess and said, '*Voila! le tableau qui se déroule à mes pieds!*' Is not this extraordinary for a child of three years old?"

The Czar Nicholas visited the Queen at Windsor in the year 1844, when she was struck by his gentle manner towards the royal children. "*Voila les doux moments de notre vie,*" he cried, when the little ones had been with their parents for a time. A speech made by the Emperor during this visit was noted by the Queen.—"Now-a-days," said the Czar, "Princes must strive to make themselves worthy of their high position, so as to reconcile the people to the fact of their being Princes."—This reminds us of the famous axiom of Frederick the Great, "The king is not the unlimited sovereign, but only the first servant of his people."—Soon after the departure of the Emperor Nicholas, the Prince of Prussia [1] arrived at Windsor on a visit. The Chevalier Bunsen, Prussian *chargé d'affaires* in London, says that the Prince then "Took an affection for England, admiring her greatness, and perceiving it to be a result of her political and religious institutions." Friendly relations sprang up at this time between the Hohenzollern Prince and Prince Albert, which time was destined to increase.

During this autumn the Queen and Prince paid their first visit to Scotland, when their eldest child accompanied them. The Queen's Highland Journal contains many records of the little traveller on her first journey.—"*Vicky* appeared as *Voyageuse*, and was all impatience to go."—When, after cruising up the east coast, the squadron had anchored off Dundee, "We got into our barge with *Vicky*. . . . . The sea was bright and blue, and we danced along beautifully. . . . Albert walked up the steps (on landing), I holding his arm, *Vicky* his hand, amidst loud cheers. . . . Our dear child behaved like a grown-up person, not put out, or frightened, or nervous. . . . At Dunkeld we stopped to let *Vicky* have some broth; she stood and bowed to the people out of the window. . . . There never was so good a traveller, sleeping in the carriage at her usual hours, not frightened by noise or crowds, pleased and amused by everything."

[1] The present Emperor of Germany (1886).

It was during this sojourn at Blair Castle that the Queen and Prince had their first refreshing experience of the benefit to be gained from the pure air of the Highlands.—" This primitive yet romantic mountain life acts like a tonic to the nerves, and gladdens the heart," the Prince wrote to Baron Stockmar, when telling him of the rosy looks of the little Princess while in Scotland.

This holiday, however, soon came to an end. For the first time in our history a reigning French monarch was to visit " the Majesty of England," and the Queen returned to Windsor in October to receive King Louis Philippe.

The Princess Royal, we hear, goes with her parents to visit this bland and courteous old gentleman in the apartments assigned for his use at Windsor. Knowing her French so well, the bright little Princess makes, doubtless, her own shrewd comments as she listens to the converse of the older folk, for she is growing very wise, living always in that great world of which history is made, and which is so full of stimulus to a large brain and quick intelligence.

" This wonderfully wise *Prinzesschen* and her merry little brother delighted to break away from the nursery, and spend a confidential twilight hour with their dear old friend, Baron Stockmar," says his son, in the *Denkwürdigkeiten*, where we find the following little story of the *Prinzesschen*. " The

Queen was reading to her little daughter one day from the Bible, when she came to the words, 'And God created man in His own image.' Already imbued, it would seem, with some perception of artistic beauty, the Princess exclaimed, 'But, mamma, *surely* not also *Doctor* . . . . ?'" "The Doctor," the Baron used to add dryly, "was *not* a handsome man. He was, in fact, excessively plain."

In 1845 "Mamma and Papa" are setting out for another delightful autumn excursion, when they are to visit "Papa's" own native Germany, and it seems very hard to their little daughter that she should be left behind.

One beautiful August morning she is standing by the Queen, who is dressing for her journey. Looking up with great, wistful eyes, the tears kept bravely back, the little Princess asks, anxiously, "But *why* am I not going to Germany?"—"Most gladly would I have taken her, but the journey is a formidable one for one so young," writes the Queen.—"What however decides us, is the visit to the King of Prussia, when I could not have looked after her myself. . . . Poor little Vicky! She seemed very sorry, yet she did not cry. It was a very painful moment when we drove away, leaving the poor little things standing at the hall door (at Osborne).—God bless them, and preserve them! They are in excellent hands."

Two years previously Lady Lyttelton had been appointed Superintendent of the Royal Nurseries. In their solicitude that from its very commencement their children's education might be conducted on the best possible method, the Queen and Prince Consort had taken counsel with their wise and faithful old friend, Baron Stockmar.—"Education," he had said, "cannot begin too soon. We must try first to regulate the natural instincts, and give them a right direction—above all things we must keep their minds pure. This can only be done by placing those persons about our children who are themselves pure and good. Children are apt to imitate whatever they may see or hear, and a living example is worth much mere precept."

The Baron therefore advised that a lady of rank and high attainments should, if possible, be placed in charge of children and teachers alike, and given that authority of personal supervision which the Queen's engrossing public duties precluded her from exercising over the details of her children's daily lives. Lady Lyttelton, who had been lady-in-waiting to the Queen for some years past, and who was admirably fitted for so responsible an office, was fortunately at liberty to accept it, and to retain it for eight years.

When at last she began to feel that she was "old enough to be at rest," "It was," says Sir Theodore Martin, "with sad hearts and tearful eyes that her young charges parted from her." Lady Lyttelton's last interview with the Queen is thus described by herself: " . . . I quite broke down, and could neither speak nor hear. I remember the Prince's face, pale as ashes, and a few words of praise and thanks; but it is all misty. . . . "

The Queen has, from time to time, recorded her views on the more essential points relating to her children's education. In a memorandum written for the guidance of the Princess Royal's instructors, her Majesty dwells on the training of the *heart* as being of all things paramount. She considers also the question of the Princess's religious instruction very anxiously. The Queen's conviction is that this is best given day by day at the mother's knee; but she writes in 1844, "Already, it is a hard case for me that my occupations prevent my being with her (the Princess Royal) when she says her prayers." Both the Queen and Prince Consort were vigilant that their children's minds might not be warped by any extreme or dogmatic systems of belief. The Queen says—" I am quite clear that the Princess should be taught to have a great reverence for God and for religion; but she should have the feeling of devotion and love, which our Heavenly Father encourages His earthly children to cherish for Him, not one of fear and trembling; that the thought of death and an after life should not be presented in an alarming, or forbidding aspect; that she should as yet be made to know no difference of creeds; that she is not to think that she can only pray on her knees, or that those who do not kneel are the less fervent and devout in their prayers."

At the risk of repeating what many may have read, I must add a few sentences taken from a touching and important record of Prince Albert's character and opinions, written by his tutor and life-long friend, Herr Florschütz, and published by General Grey, in his " Early years of the Prince Consort." The Prince's convictions on vital questions are so essentially those of his daughter, as expressed in her efforts for the good of her fellow-men, that they cannot well be omitted here.

" His was no lip service, his faith was essentially one of the heart, a living faith, giving impulse to his whole life. Deeply embued with the great truths of Christianity, his religion went far beyond all forms. To these, indeed, he attached no especial importance. The spirit, as distinguished from the letter, was his constant and unerring guide."

In harmony with these words is the following extract from " Woman's Work," by Amelie Sohr, a book which embodies the thoughts, and even the words of the Crown Princess on many all-important subjects. Speaking of the work of nursing the sick, this book says:

"The rules and outward observances of any religious profession must exercise a prejudicial influence over work which demands for its efficient fulfilment our best strength and energy. . . . There is need of no higher proof of the sincerity of the religious convictions than the choice of this calling" (the calling of nurse to the sick poor), "which is not to be conceived of as existing deprived of Christian love. . . . The essence of true religion must inspire every good and disciplined woman . . . who makes choice of this arduous and self-denying vocation."

Lady Lyttelton once heard a conversation between Prince Albert and one of the lords-in-waiting which she noted down as characteristic. On the occasion of the birth of one of the Queen's children the Prince was asked whether an additional prayer might not be added to the morning service.—"No, no, you pray for the Queen five times already—it is too much," said the Prince.

"*Can* we pray too much for her Majesty, sir?"

"Not too *fervently*, but too often," was the reply of the Prince.

During the spring of 1845, the estate of Osborne was purchased by the Queen, where, in the pure air and seclusion of the Isle of Wight, the royal children might gain health and freedom for the cultivation of those simple, natural tastes, so dear to both their parents. While, from its fertile soil and great natural beauties, Osborne gave to Prince Albert scope for the exercise of his favourite occupations, farming and landscape-gardening, it afforded the royal family good sea-bathing, and—"A home of their own,"—as the Queen calls it, when telling the King of the Belgians of her purchase. We smile to think of the "lady of all the land" as hitherto possessing no *home*, forgetting that the royal palaces belong to the nation.

Here, happy, busy little Princes and Princesses had soon created for themselves a little paradise of gardens and bowers. Here they could sow and reap, dig and water, to their hearts' content. A Swiss cottage, full grown and capacious, was given to them by their father, to become the treasure-house for all those collections of flowers, and shells, and butterflies, and stones, so dear to the heart of every simply-educated child.

This delightful Swiss cottage possessed a real cooking-stove, kitchen utensils, china closet, small brooms and brushes, to be "plied by busy house-wives" when they awaited, with hospitable pride, those parental visitors who often came there to see them. These little cooks, when they invited illustrious guests to lunch with them, prepared all the dishes with their own nimble fingers. Once they received a very learned sage in their island home, a great chemist, who had come from a far-off land to visit Prince Albert. Baron Liebig afterwards told his friends how charmingly he was entertained by the royal children when he spent a happy day at Osborne. His little hosts led him about, showing him their treasures; they baked a little cake for him, then and there, using, doubtless, such small crucibles as were not unfamiliar to their guest, and this cake was eaten with quite a peculiar relish, as we may well suppose.

A pretty picture comes before our eyes—grave science entering with zest into the simple joys of youth. Perhaps that kind royal lady who has so much pleasure in seeing miniature laundresses and cooks intent upon their happy play-work in the Pestalozzi-Fröbel house in Berlin, may recall the occupations of her own childhood, as she plans similar useful pleasures for the infant scholars of her adopted country.

"We both always say to one another," writes the Princess Alice to the Queen, when visiting her sister at Potsdam, "that no children ever were so happy, so spoilt with all the comforts and enjoyments that children could wish for, as we were."

Pleasant as their island home might be, it was thought well to leave it for a more bracing climate during the autumn months. Balmoral was, in 1847, not as yet purchased by Prince Albert, but Ardverikie, on the west coast of Inverness-shire, had been taken, and here, amongst the great mountains they loved so well, rest was sought for a time.

The wise and kindly hill folk of North Britain know well how to respect the privacy of their neighbours. Their common sense and "breeding" must be as refreshing to those who seek repose from public life, as are the crisp air, the grey rocks, the purple heather, and the silent company of great Bens, standing round the straths and glens in the north country. "Is this the Queen's carriage coming?" I once said to a man standing by the half-door of his little shop in the "street" of Braemar. "Hir Maijistie dis'na care to have folk glowerin' at her ower mickle," replied this Highland gentleman, and he turned away from the approaching wagonette, as well as from the querist, leaving her to realize her inferiority in good manners.

VI.

GIRLHOOD OF THE PRINCESS ROYAL.

(1847-1858.)

> "*Truth shall nurse her,*
> *Holy and heavenly thoughts still counsel her.*"
> KING HENRY VIII.

DURING the autumn of 1847 Prince Albert's thoughts were painfully engrossed by the state of Germany. He could foresee the dangers which were then imminent, and was eager to point out to the rulers of continental states the necessity, so evident to himself, for granting voluntarily those righteous reforms which were sure to be wrested from them ultimately by bloodshed and violence. Viewed by the light of after events, and in connection with the close alliance which was to bind England and Germany together at a later period, we may still read with instruction and interest the statement of Prince Albert's wise, far-seeing views, to be found in the pages of his Life.

Prussia was virtually governed in 1847 by an irresponsible minister. Manteuffel was all powerful, the Prince of Prussia powerless to induce his brother, the King, to listen to the just demands of his people. The father of the future Crown Princess of Germany had also tried vainly to awaken the sovereigns of the German States to a sense of their responsibilities. He, like the Prince of Prussia, found himself unable to influence the course of events. His worst fears were too soon justified, and his heart wrung by the accounts which began to be frequent of the conflicts between the authorities and the people of Germany.

Matters grew still more threatening as the winter advanced. Early in 1848 the Revolution in France was the precursor of similar spectacles in almost every European State. England and Belgium alone stood firm, secure in their constitutional government, while kings were flying from their insurgent people in Germany, Austria, and Spain. Prince Albert was constantly harassed and distressed by this condition of things in his native land; and his health was beginning to suffer from the long strain of hard work. Yet it was during the spring of 1848 that his first great public speech was made—a speech which excited the admiration of the whole country by its large benevolence and wisdom. Speaking on behalf of the Society for the Improvement of Artisans'.

Dwellings, the Prince said,—" The interests of classes, too often contrasted, are identical. It is ignorance alone which prevents them meeting for their mutual benefit. To dispel that ignorance, to show how man can help man, notwithstanding the complicated state of civilized society, ought to be the aim of every philanthropic person."—These words so exactly express the ideas of the Crown Princess, as shown in her efforts for the people of her adopted country, that they may fitly appear in any record of her life and work.

Prince Albert wrote on one occasion to Colonel Phipps that there were—" Four things which he should never cease to promote, with a view to the improvement of the condition of the working classes. First, the education of the children with industrial training;[1] second, the improvement of their dwellings;[2] third, that allotments be given with the cottages; fourth, the encouragement of savings-banks and benefit societies, managed, if possible, by themselves, and on sound economical principles."—

" If all the cottage property in the kingdom were kept in the same condition as that of the Queen and Prince Consort, the death rate would be

[1] *Comp.* the Industrial Schools in Berlin, which have the support of the Crown Princess.
[2] The Princess is protector of the association in Berlin which answers to our Sanitary Society for house to house visiting.

reduced by nearly one half," said Mr. Chadwick in his report on the condition of the dwellings of the poor. Lady Lyttelton has stated that during winter and hard weather the labourers on the estate at Osborne were always kept on, while they were at liberty to seek harvesting or other well-paid work when it was offered to them elsewhere. During the building of the new castle at Balmoral the same beneficent rule was followed, and work pushed on at those seasons when the workmen most needed it.

Balmoral was occupied experimentally in 1848, with a view to its purchase in the following year. Sir James Clark had pronounced the district between Aboyne and Castleton of Braemar to be especially suited to the constitutions of the royal family, and here, with the light mountain air they were to breathe-in health and good spirits for many happy years to come. In a country where the poorest cottager is self-respecting and independent, the children might learn to know "the short and simple annals of the poor," without fear of pauperizing their cottage friends; and here, too, like Sir Walter of the Border, they could learn to "look upon a blue mountain as a friend."—The present writer ventures to rank this last as an important factor in the education of the young.—

The Prince made an important address on behalf of the Servants' Provident and Benevolent

Society in the autumn of 1848. He was anxious to promote thrift amongst persons too prone to extravagance, as he had been struck by the fact that a large proportion of the older occupants of our workhouses had once been domestic servants. The words and thoughts of her father always sank deep into the mind of his eldest daughter, who had, from her earliest years, been his frequent companion. The Prince delighted in her quick intelligence and lively mind. While she was but a child he had permitted her to comprehend something of those pursuits which most interested him, and which she was soon able to enter into with eager pleasure. She often accompanied her father in his walks, when he taught her to know every "herb and plant which drinks the dew," by its English, German, and Latin name.

The Princess, with her sister and two brothers, accompanied the Queen and Prince when their long-deferred visit was paid to Ireland in the summer of 1849. Lady Lyttleton, watching the Royal squadron from the windows at Osborne, as it steamed down the English Channel, exclaimed: "It is done! England's fate is afloat, and we are left lamenting!" When so intelligent and cultivated a woman as Lady Lyttleton could regard the visit of our Sovereign to her warm-hearted Irish subjects with so much dread, we may guess what was then the popular feeling in England with regard to the sister isle. But any doubt of their loyalty would have seemed strange to the poor people who were just then making ready so enthusiastic a welcome for " the lady of *their* land."

No people on the face of the round earth are *by nature* more loyal—loyal, above all, to a Queen, a woman, than the Irish, and this they proved convincingly in the year 1849. The Queen has all the courage of her race, and she could feel no fear, although the English press had done its best to create a panic amongst her English subjects, by publishing exaggerated reports of the state of Ireland. The royal squadron entered the Cove of Cork, thenceforth to be called Queenstown, one lovely summer's evening, when the "pleasant waters of the river Lee" were reflecting the light of countless bonfires blazing on all the surrounding hills.—" The peasants, wild with delight, piled turf, faggot, and tar-barrel, higher and higher, to give earnest of their welcome; but this was only a prelude to the enthusiastic loyalty which hailed the Royal visitors at every stage of their progress."

"A wonderful, striking spectacle," is the Queen's comment on this greeting of her Irish subjects. " It was a noble and stirring spectacle," Her Majesty goes on to say, when the great vessels had glided up the beautiful bay of Dublin, and the Royal party had landed at Kingstown pier. *The Times*, in its report, says:—" Ladies, throwing aside the old form of waving handkerchiefs, cheered for their lives, . . while the men rent the air with shouts of joy."—The Royal children were everywhere the objects of the warmest interest and admiration.—" O ! *Queen dear*," cried one poor woman, " call one of them Patrick, and we'll all die for you !" Our good Queen did indeed name her next son Arthur Patrick, after her old and venerated friend, an Irish hero, and after Ireland's saint. — " The presence of the Queen will have produced more good here than in any other part of her dominions," —wrote Lord Clarendon (then Lord Lieutenant of Ireland) to Sir George Grey, when the squadron was anchored in Belfast Lough. From thence it proceeded, in a violent storm, to Glasgow, whence Balmoral was reached in the course of a few days.

Soon after the return of the Royal Family to London, the Princess Royal made her first public appearance in the City of London. The Queen was at that time suffering from chicken pox, and was unable to perform the ceremony of opening the new Coal Exchange in the City of London. Prince Albert, representing Her Majesty, took barge with his two eldest children, at Westminster, on a beautiful October morning in 1849, and was rowed down the river by twenty-seven watermen, to Blackfriars Pier. On landing—"The scene was magnificent, delightful to see and hear," wrote Lady Lyttelton to Mrs. Gladstone on the following day.—" The cheers close to us as we passed up the covered way, every one looking so *affectionately*, quite like parents, on the two little creatures, stretching over each other's shoulders to smile at them. . . I shall never forget it. . . A striking thing is that *loyalty*. How strong and deep it is here in England!"—A clergyman who was present on that occasion, described it to me lately, unconscious of my peculiar interest in it. He could still see, he said, the little upright, queenly figure of the Princess Royal, her pretty bows, and bright smiles, as—undismayed by the deafening plaudits of the people—she held her father's hand, and glanced from face to face. A glad, radiant, look came into her eyes, it seemed as if some chord of sympathy was vibrating within her, and stirring her consciousness of human kinship with all those jubilant and kindly people.—

On their northern journey in the autumn of 1850, the Queen and Prince, with their two eldest daughters, halted at Edinburgh, to occupy the rooms in the ancient Holyrood Palace, which had not been used by a sovereign of Great Britain since the days of the beautiful Queen Mary. So inspired were they by the romance of the spot, that they—" Wandered out with the two girls,"—

to quote from the "Leaves from the Journal of our Life in the Highlands,"—"to explore the ruined abbey," without waiting to rest after their journey. We may easily suppose that her first sight of the romantic capital of Scotland would become a "joy for ever" to so bright and precocious a girl as the Princess Royal. Though she was then scarcely ten years old, we must recollect that she was already the companion of a father who had been, if one may so express it, *brought up* upon Sir Walter Scott. In the delightful record of Prince Albert's childhood, a clever and warm-hearted grandmother often appears, who was in the habit of relating the stories of Sir Walter Scott's novels towards bedtime to two eager, bright-eyed little grandsons, as they sat by her knee, gazing up into her kind face. What pictures might the "big blue eyes of Albertchen" have seen while they were fixed dreamily on the features he loved so well! When drinking in those tales of Scottish chivalry which fill every inch of the north country with romance, did he ever, perchance, see himself sharing the throne of a gentle cousin, who was one day to hold sway over that enchanted land?

"The girls climbed the castle rock *incog.*," proceeds the Queen's Journal.—As they gazed from those old battlements, the faint blue outline of the Highland hills fringing the horizon, the Firth and

Inchkeith lying below them, they could discern the battle-fields where many a stout fight had been headed by their ancestors. Here every name might recall a story whose hero was of their own ancient lineage.

Our happy young Princess was busily occupied, during the years which followed, in building up the edifice of a solid and comprehensive education. In addition to the usual studies of her age, pursued under the direction of able professors, she enjoyed a rare educational influence in the constant sympathy of her father. That such a close association with the Prince Consort was not only intellectually, but morally inspiring, it is needless to say. It was his custom, when she was barely thirteen, to impart to her the contents of letters embracing a political correspondence with every country of the civilized world, and to show her copies of his replies. Special subjects were added to her course of study, such as national economy: in which apparently dry science Mr. Ellis was her instructor, whose books are said to combine, "tenderness of feeling with a severely disciplined judgment." We may hope that they proved less severe than their titles would imply.—"Vicky is also very busy," the Prince Consort once wrote to Prince Frederick William during the period of his engagement—" she is learning many and various things. She comes to me every evening from six to seven, when I put her through a kind of general catechising. In order to make her ideas clear I let her work out subjects for herself, which she then brings to me for correction. She is at present writing a short compendium of Roman history."

During the autumn previous to her marriage, the Prince Consort had given his daughter the difficult task of translating a German pamphlet which had recently been published at Weimar. It was a work full of condensed power, and dealt with the past and future of German policy in a broad and liberal spirit, being full of ideas such as would inspire the future sovereign of a great nation with a just and right ambition. So well was this work translated that the Prince lent the manuscript to Lord Clarendon for his perusal. In returning it, Lord Clarendon expressed his admiration of the clearness with which the writer's ideas had been rendered in English, and proceeded to say, " The Princess's manner would not be what it is if it were not the reflection of a highly cultivated intellect, which, with a well-trained imagination, leads to the saying and doing of right things in the right places. In reading Droysen (the pamphleteer) I felt that the motto of Prussia should be *semper eadem*, and in thinking of his translator I felt that she is destined to change that motto into the *vigilando ascendimus* of Weimar."

The spring of 1854 opened ominously for England. An ancient Cambridge prediction has it that, "When our Lord falls in our Lady's lap, then will come England's mishap." The reading of this mystic saying being, that when Lady-day and Good Friday both fall on the 25th of March evil will follow for our country. Strange to say this happened in 1854, when the Crimean War was imminent.

Mr. Kinglake has told the story of that war with terribly dramatic force, setting down every blunder remorselessly, bringing tears to the eyes by his record of the bitter privations, the heroic endurance of our brave troops. What was the agony then endured by wives and mothers? What was the distress of our Queen and Prince, better informed all along, and more fully aware than we, of the sufferings endured by their soldiers, and powerless to avert or mitigate them? Yet from the black chaos of battle and pestilence rise up the forms of Florence Nightingale and her band of devoted helpers, bringing peace to the dying, ease to the wounded; setting such "sweet Amens to hideous deeds" as might go far to atone for the horrors of war. For do not all our hospital and nursing reforms date from the close of the Crimean War, just as many of the nursing *Vereins* in Germany date from the Austrian Campaign of 1866?

Miss Nightingale visited the Queen at Balmoral

at the close of the war, when she did not shrink from laying before her Majesty the evils of the existing hospital system, nor hesitate when asked by the Prince Consort to suggest a scheme for the needed reforms. The Princess Royal then received her first impulse towards that branch of female work, which now, of all others, has such strong interest for her; that work which she organized during the anxious winter of the great Franco-German war with such admirable success. It is known that our two eldest Princesses—children though they still were—often longed and even planned together to join Miss Nightingale in the East in those days, hearing as they did so constantly of the sufferings of the soldiers.

One pleasant consequence of the French coalition with England was a visit paid by our Queen and Prince and their eldest daughter to Paris, in the summer of 1855. No pains were spared to show these important guests Paris *en fête*, while the city was bathed in sunshine, gay, beautiful, and apparently prosperous. Our young Princess entered into all the delight of a first visit to the French capital with the fresh zest of her age and character. The Empress was then at the zenith of her power and beauty, and filled her high position with grace and tact. She was charmed with the natural enjoyment expressed by her young guest.—"The Empress parted from Vicky very sorrowfully"—

the Queen records at the conclusion of the visit, and she describes a magnificent bracelet set with rubies and diamonds, and containing a lock of hair, which was the parting gift of this charming woman to our English Princess.

Within a month of the return of the Royal party from France, the news of the fall of Sebastopol was flashed to the Queen at Balmoral. When the shades of evening fell, a huge bonfire was kindled on Craig Gowan to proclaim the tidings to all the neighbouring glens.—" It illuminated all the peaks round about, and the scattered population of the valleys, understanding the signal, made for the mountain, where we performed a veritable witch's dance round the flames, supported by whisky,"— wrote the Prince Consort to Baron Stockmar, early in September. On the 13th of the same month he wrote again to tell his old friend that "Prince Fritz William of Prussia" was to arrive on the following day.

Later letters speak of this guest as "free from prejudices and pre-eminently well-intentioned," and say that his "leading characteristics are great straightforwardness, frankness, and honesty." When at last, after a visit of several weeks, the young Prussian Prince had left Balmoral, Prince Albert opened his heart to that faithful friend whose devotion to his "wonderfully wise *Prinzesschen*" is so well known, and told the Baron of the event which had occurred. After speaking of the youth of the Princess, and the reluctance of the Queen that she should be disturbed by such ideas as those which had been confided by Prince Frederick William to her parents; after relating that incident already quoted in Chapter IV., which led to the discovery of the mutual attachment of the young people, the Prince goes on to say,—" Vicky has indeed behaved quite admirably during the closer explanation of Saturday, as well as in the self-command she has shown since and at parting. She has manifested towards Fritz and ourselves the most childlike candour and simplicity, as well as the best feeling."

In tracing the outline of Prince Frederick William's life during the two years which intervened between his betrothal and his marriage, it has been possible also to give some incidents in the life of the Princess Royal, for the Prince was able to visit England frequently, and to join in the joys and sorrows of the Princess constantly during their engagement. An occurrence has been mentioned in a previous chapter, which must have impressed the Princess deeply.

While the Queen was bestowing the Victoria Cross on the brave men who had fought for her in the Crimea, she was in great anxiety about her troops in India. In June accounts of the disaffection of the native population were already beginning to excite alarm throughout the whole Empire, and too soon the frightful details of the Indian Mutiny were filling England with horror and dismay. During the autumn before her marriage the Princess Royal shared the grief and solicitude of her parents, as heartrending accounts were coming to them with such frequency of the fate of English men, women, and children in that far-off portion of the British Empire. As the winter approached, Sir Colin Campbell succeeded in turning the course of events. His relief of Lucknow needs no comment here. It was the subject of a touching picture painted by the Princess Royal before her marriage, and it was most undoubtedly a great addition to her happiness at this period to know that she need no longer think anxiously of the fate of her countrymen in the East. A beautiful letter, addressed by the Queen to Sir Colin Campbell a few days before the wedding festivities began, will show the feeling of the royal family towards the heroes of the Mutiny.

"The Queen must herself give utterance to the feelings of pride and satisfaction with which she has heard of the glorious victories which Sir Colin Campbell and the heroic troops which he has under his command have obtained over the mutineers. The manner in which Sir Colin has conducted all the operations, and his rescue of that devoted band of heroes and heroines at Lucknow (which brought comfort and relief to so many anxious hearts) are beyond all praise. The Queen has had many proofs already of Sir Colin's devotion to his sovereign and his country, and he has now greatly added to that debt of gratitude which both owe to him. But Sir Colin must bear one reproof from his Queen, and that is that he exposes himself too much. His life is most precious, and she entreats that he will neither put himself where his noble spirit would urge him to be—foremost in danger—nor fatigue himself so as to injure his health. In this anxious wish the Prince most earnestly joins, as well as in all the Queen's previous expressions.

"That so many gallant and brave and distinguished men, beginning with one whose name will ever be remembered with pride, viz., General Havelock, should have fallen, is a great grief to the Queen. To all European, as well as native troops, who have fought so nobly, and so gallantly, and amongst whom the Queen is rejoiced to see the 93rd, the Queen wishes Sir Colin to convey the expression of her great admiration and gratitude.

"The Queen cannot conclude without sending Sir Colin the congratulations and good wishes of our dear daughter the Princess Royal, who is in a fortnight to leave her native land. The Queen concludes with the fervent wish that the

God of battles may ever attend and protect Sir Colin and his noble army."

When the Princess Royal said good-bye to the cottagers by Deeside, in the October preceding her marriage, tears were shed and there were sad hearts amongst the simple kindly people she had so often visited.—"And will we ever see you again?" many are said to have asked.—Years later these people used to follow the course of the Franco-German war with keen interest, knowing that the two Princesses they had watched growing into womanhood were then feeling all the anguish and suspense of the devoted wife, when her husband has gone to face danger in defence of hearth and home.

But for the present our concern is with peaceful and joyful events only.

VII.

THE ROYAL MARRIAGE.

(January 25, 1858.)

> *O when her life was yet in bud,*
> *He, too, foretold the perfect rose,*
> *For thee she grew, for thee she grows*
> *For ever, and as fair as good.*
>
> IN MEMORIAM.

PRINCE Frederick William left Berlin on the 21st of January, crossed the Channel in the yacht *Vivid*, and reached Buckingham Palace on the 23rd. The Prince and Princess of Prussia, with numerous other royal personages, had been the guests of the Queen and Prince Consort for some days previously, when " from eighty to ninety persons sat down to dinner at the royal table daily." On the 19th, a performance of Macbeth, with Miss Helen Faucit and Mr. Phelps in the principal parts, had taken place by the Queen's request at Her Majesty's Theatre. The house was beautifully decorated with flowers, and the divisions beween the boxes of the grand tier had been removed for the convenience of that "wonderful row of royalties" mentioned in the Queen s Diary of this date. After the concluding comedy, in which Mr. and Mrs. Keeley appeared, the whole house rose, and "God save the Queen" was sung, amidst a spectacle such as could certainly not have found a parallel in Europe.

A state ball was held on the following evening, when, says Herr Hengst, "The bride was the centre of all interest and sympathy. Her charming freshness, her grace and her *esprit*, were the delight of all who were present."

Contemporary accounts give the details of the splendid ceremonial of the Royal Wedding, but Sir Theodore Martin has also been permitted to publish some passages from the diaries of the Queen which present its deeper aspects, while showing the tender mother's heart filled with loving solicitude for her young daughter, as she saw her going forth bravely, lovingly, from the warm protecting arms which had been so close around her through all her happy childhood, to meet her new and most responsible duties. The Queen knew how well-fitted her daughter was for the exalted sphere she was about to fill; she was trusting her treasure, too, to one who would cherish it nobly, and who possessed her perfect trust. We can trace this assurance in every allusion to the Crown Prince throughout the large volumes of the Prince Consort's Life.

On the 24th the Queen and Prince had themselves arranged the wedding presents for the young pair in the great drawing-room at Buckingham Palace:—" Mama's and ours on one table; Fritz's, his parents', the King's and Queen's [of Prussia], Uncle's,[1] and Ernest's and Alexandrine's,[2] on the other. . . Fritz's pearls were the largest I have ever seen, one row. On a third table were three fine candelabra, our gift to Fritz. . . We brought in Fritz and Vicky; she was in ecstacies — quite startled — Fritz delighted. . . Service at half-past eleven. The Bishop of Oxford preached a fine sermon. . . After luncheon we went to the present-room again, where we found more fine gifts had been placed, many from ladies, including a quantity of work. . . Dear Vicky gave me a brooch (a very pretty one) before church, with her hair, and clasping me in her arms said, " I hope to be worthy to be your child!"

On the 25th the Queen records,—" While dressing, dearest Vicky came to me, looking well and composed, and in a fine quiet frame of mind. . . Then came the time to go. The sun was shining

[1] The King of the Belgians.
[2] The Duke and Duchess of Saxe Coburg-Gotha.

brightly; thousands had been out since very early, shouting, bells ringing, etc. Albert, and uncle in Field-marshal's uniform with bâtons, and the two eldest boys went first. Then the three girls, in pink satin trimmed with Newport lace; Alice with a wreath, and the two others with only bouquets in their hair of cornflowers—the favourite flower of Queen Louise [1] and all her descendants—and marguerites. The flourish of trumpets, and cheering of thousands, made my heart sink within me. Vicky was in the carriage with me, sitting opposite. . . At St. James's I took her into a dressing-room prettily arranged, where were uncle, Albert, and the eight bridesmaids, who looked charming, in white tulle, with wreaths and bouquets of roses and white heather. . . Fritz looked pale and much agitated, but behaved with the greatest self-possession. . . . Our darling Flower looked very touching and lovely, with such an innocent, confiding, and serious expression, her veil hanging back over her shoulders, walking between her beloved father and dearest uncle Leopold. . . My last fear of being overcome vanished, on seeing Vicky's calm and composed manner. It was beautiful to see her kneeling with Fritz, their hands joined, her eight maidens looking like a cloud hovering near her. . . . Fritz spoke very plainly, Vicky too; the Archbishop omitted some

[1] Of Prussia.

passages of the service. When the ceremony was over, we both embraced Vicky tenderly, but she shed not one tear. . . . She then went to her new parents, we too crossing over to the dear Prince and Princess, who were both much moved ; I kissing both, and pressing their hands with a most happy feeling. My heart was so full. . . . The bride and bridegroom left hand in hand. . . .

" On arriving at the palace we went with the young couple to the celebrated window[1] at which they stepped out and showed themselves, we and the Prince and Princess (of Prussia) standing with them."

After the wedding-breakfast, the bridal pair drove to the Paddington station, and left for Windsor, from whence a letter arrived in the evening, telling that the Eton boys had met them at the station, and dragged their carriage up the steep hill to the Castle, with ringing cheers. That night London was brilliantly illuminated, and a State concert closed the eventful day.

The brief honeymoon lasted but two days, the Court removing to Windsor on the 27th, when the bridegroom was invested with the Order of the Garter, and a State banquet was held in the Waterloo Chamber. By the 30th the Royal Family

[1] The window over the central archway leading to the courtyard.

were again at Buckingham Palace, where addresses, gifts, and tokens of affectionate loyalty, were pouring in from every town in the Kingdom. A monster Drawing-room was held, and the Prince and Princess Frederick William went in state to the Opera.

Amid the occupations of the wedding day, Prince Albert had found time to write to Baron Stockmar, whose absence, from illness, had then been much deplored. The Baron's son had arrived alone some days previously ("But this is not our own Baron," little Prince Leopold said to Miss Hillyard, his governess, on seeing him), and was to accompany the Princess Royal to Berlin, as a member of her household. Prince Albert felt that "the recollections of forty years," must have been awakened in his old friend's heart by all that was then occurring in England.—"It is just eighteen years since you were present in the Chapel Royal at my marriage with Victoria," he wrote to the Baron.—"Uncle Leopold, whom you accompanied to London forty years ago,[1] on the occasion of his marriage [with the Princess Charlotte], will be one of the bride's supporters to-day. These reminiscences must excite a special feeling within you to-day, with which I hope is coupled the conviction that we all gratefully revere in you a dear friend and wise counsellor."

[1] Now nearly 70 years ago.

Writing to the Dowager Duchess of Saxe-Coburg a few days later, the Prince said,—" The separation for ever of our dear daughter from the family circle will make a frightful gap in our hearts. I do not trust myself to think of Tuesday (the day of departure of the Princess). . . . In Germany, people seem prepared to welcome her with the greatest friendliness. Here the love and enthusiasm of the people are not to be described; they are quite touching."

—" The thought of the separation hangs," says the Queen's diary, "like a storm over us! But God will carry us through it, and we have the comfort of seeing the young people so perfectly happy." Her Majesty's brief entry on the Monday is, " The last day of our dear child's being with us, which is incredible, and makes me feel at times quite sick at heart."—" I think it will kill me to take leave of dear papa," were the words of the Princess to her mother at this time.

On the Tuesday, after speaking of an early morning interview with her dear daughter, the Queen goes on to say,—" And now the dreadful time was at hand. . . As I came down the stairs my breaking heart gave way. . . The hall was full. . . I do not think there was a dry eye. . . I clasped her in my arms and blessed her, and knew not what to say. I kissed good Fritz and pressed his hand again and again. He was unable to speak, and the tears were in his eyes. . . Albert got into the carriage — an open one — with them and Bertie (the Prince of Wales). . . A dreadful moment, and a dreadful day. Such sickness came over me, real heartache, when I thought of our dearest child being gone. . . It began to snow before Vicky went, and continued to do so without intermission all the day. . . At four my beloved Albert returned. The separation had been dreadful. . . Nothing could exceed the loyal enthusiasm and feeling shown by the countless thousands in the city, and again at Gravesend, where the decorations were beautiful. In spite of the snow, young girls with wreaths walked on the pier scattering flowers. . . Albert had waited to see the ship leave."

On the following day the Prince Consort wrote to his daughter, "I am not of a demonstrative nature, and therefore you can hardly know how dear you have always been to me, and what a void you leave behind in my heart — yet not in my heart, for there assuredly you will abide henceforth as till now you have done — but in my daily life, which is ever reminding my heart of your absence."

Writing to Baron Stockmar the Prince says, "Throughout all this agitating, serious, and very trying time, the good child has behaved quite admirably, and to the mingled admiration and surprise of every one. She has been so natural, so childlike, so dignified and firm in her whole bearing and demeanour, that one might well believe in a higher inspiration... Of the touching sympathy and enthusiasm of all ranks of the people you can form no conception. Even by the humblest cottagers her marriage was regarded as if it were their own family affair." A few days later he writes to his daughter,—" Thank God, everything apparently goes on to a wish, and you seem to win golden opinions... What has given us the most pleasure was your letter, so overflowing with affection."—

The snow fell fast on that cheerless February day when our Princess Royal was borne swiftly away over the grey waters of the German Ocean from the land of her birth,—from the large family circle whose sunshine she had been. But bright skies were awaiting her in the land of her adoption, a warm welcome was offered to the daughter of the sea-girt isle at every stage of her progress to Berlin. Passing on from Brussels—where the first night was spent by the young pair as the guests of the King of the Belgians—through a pretty, rocky district, towards the German frontier, they came to Herbesthal, where the Princess found herself at last in the Fatherland.—" The whole nation came forth to meet them, the love of a great people accompanied them as they proceeded towards home. When they came to the old, world-famous town of Aix-la-Chapelle, they were welcomed by its burghers, calling themselves "True sons of Prussia," to their ancient Council Chamber and their venerable cathedral, where thirty-six German Emperors had been crowned." As they drew near to Cologne they beheld, shining out of the blackness of night, a huge luminous minster, each pinnacle, each buttress, traced, as it were, with a pencil of fire upon the wintry sky. Here the Princess slept on German soil for the first time.—" Everything had been so disposed in her rooms as to look homelike and familiar—she might have been returning to some well-known spot after a short visit."

The young pair sped on, the following day, by many a substantial manufacturing town to Magdeburg, their next halting place. About midday they stopped for an hour at Minden, and here Frau Polko—herself a young wife then—saw them, as she can still see them photographed on her memory.—" A deputation of red-cheeked Westphalian peasant women, dressed in the costume of their province—in scarlet petticoats, black bodices, and their black head-dresses, with great strings of amber hanging round their necks, had come to present an address to the bridal pair. Close beside her tall, stalwart-looking husband, stood the little bride, her sweet child-like face flushing and paling by turns, her large clear eyes resting upon the spokeswoman. — Unser Fritz looked then the embodiment of youth, health, and happiness."

By noon on February 6th the towers of Potsdam were in sight, and here, as the train thundered across the long railway bridge and drew up at the platform, the smiling face of the Prince of Prussia presented itself to his children's sight. As the party drove through the town in state carriages to the Old Palace, the bells pealed out, great guns were discharged, and the people cheered till the welkin rang again. In the court of the palace the Princess of Prussia was waiting at the foot of the great marble steps, with many members of the Royal Family, to welcome the young bride. All the Princes and Princesses cried with one voice as she drove up,—" Welcome to Potsdam ! "

In the afternoon a reception, attended by the notable persons of the Residence, was held in the marble saloon, and when all public functions were fulfilled, it may well be supposed that the young Prince and Princess were glad to spend the evening, as the papers announced, " quietly in the family circle." The following day was Sunday. After attending divine service in the morning, the bridal pair drove to Babelsberg, the favourite home of the Prince's boyhood. This sweet place must be charming even when clad in its snowy mantle.—" When you see it," says a sprightly American writer, " you can scarcely believe that there has ever been a Fall: you look at something exquisite out of every window."—When we saw it, all its rare trees and shrubs were thick with leaf and blossom, its parterres brilliant with bloom. The house is small compared with the immense palaces lying below, by the brink of the lakes and rivers which give life to the view from all its windows. The rooms occupied by the royal family are distinguished by the simplicity of their arrangements. In this respect Babelsberg reminded us of Rheinhardtsbrunn, one of the happy homes of Prince Albert's youth in the heart of the Thuringian Forest.

Another great reception was held on the afternoon of the 7th, when the chiefs of the civil and military services and all the principal people of the vicinity were introduced to the bride. On the evening of this day many anxious looks were turned to the setting sun, many hopes expressed for a bright to-morrow, when much of the enjoyment of the great pageant which was occupying every one's thoughts would depend on fine weather.

VIII.

WELCOME TO BERLIN.
(February the 8th, 1858.)

> "'Tis well—The citizens
> Have shown at full their loyal minds
> In celebration of this day with shows,
> Pageants, and sights of honour."
> KING HENRY VIII.

THE sun rose brightly on the morning of February the 8th, and was sparkling on blade, on leaf, and frost-bound ground by nine o'clock, when the gala carriage, in which sat the young Prince and Princess, was crossing the long Havel bridge at Potsdam, preceded and followed by a splendid staff of outriders and equerries.

The country folk from all the neighbouring villages had been pouring in, dressed in their Sunday best, ever since daybreak, and were forming themselves into bands to give the bridal pair escort all the way to Berlin. When the royal *cortège* reached the Bellevue Palace, just outside the gates, it halted, for here the invalid King, regardless of his doctor's advice, was waiting with the Queen to meet and welcome his nephew and his new niece.—" How delightful that thou art here at last ! "[1] he repeated again and again, as he embraced the Princess.—When the procession had once more set forth the King returned to his quiet apartments at Charlottenburg, while the Queen hastened by a different route to the Old Palace in Berlin to surprise the young pair by appearing there to greet them with many other members of the Hohenzollern family.

Berlin had been decking itself for days past to do honour to this joyful occasion. I will borrow a few sentences from the record of an eye-witness, which may help to bring the scene before us. "The sun was shining out of a cloudless blue sky; countless flags and banners fluttered in the fresh morning breeze; the scaffoldings which had arisen in all the wider streets and squares were bright with crimson cloth and green branches, and filled with well-dressed ladies. The foot passengers in holiday garb, who were thronging every space, brought an enthusiasm, a warmth of feeling, to this great spectacle that was quite touching, almost overpowering to witness. Every house had

[1] "Wie herrlich dass du endlich hier bist !"

hung out gay-coloured stuffs and flags, and was garlanded with green; not only were windows and balconies crowded with expectant faces, the very roofs were covered with people. The air was filled with the clanging of bells and the hum of voices, broken, at short intervals, by the roar of the great guns.

"The city guilds had come forth to the number of 30,000 souls, with bands playing and flags flying, to meet the royal pair. As the stately cavalcade neared the Brandenburg Gate the children of the city orphanages strewed flowers before the carriage of the Prince and Princess, singing the national hymn in their clear childish voices. At the Gate itself, the chiefs of the civil and military departments, with the veteran Field-Marshal von Wrangel at their head, were waiting to receive them. Addresses were presented, replies made, as they passed slowly along the Pariser Platz.[1] Here a salvo of artillery was fired, and the bells rang out tumultuously, yet both were overpowered by the resounding huzzahs of the multitude.

"It was two o'clock before the Old Palace was descried, across the fine bridge spanning the river Spree, which leads into the Museum Platz. The groups of sculptured figures adorning this bridge were draped with flowers and garlands, while

[1] *Platz* is Square or Place in German.

the colossal bronze equestrian statue of the great Frederick shone in the bright rays of the sun high above the heads of the people. When the court of the Old Palace was reached, the whole of the royal family came forth to welcome and embrace the 'Heir to the Hohenzollern throne, and the Princess from the sea-girt isle.'—Three times did the bride come out on the balcony, in response to the cheering of the vast crowd filling the Museum Platz below."

At four o'clock a state banquet was served in the famous White Saloon, where the stony forms of the Brandenburg Kurfürsts stand round between white marble pillars, while Rauch's beautiful "Victoria," lightly poised on her pedestal, at the end of this immense hall, seems about to soar heavenward from their midst. The lights from countless crystal chandeliers[1] were reflected from the gold and silver, the jewels, stars, and orders of the guests around the great table, as well as from the mirror-like floor of this splendid chamber, which resembles a fine inlaid table.

When night had come, Berlin was suddenly bathed in a sea of light. No one was too poor to place a rushlight in the window-pane, while the wealthy had set those four wax-lights between each double casement which when lighted produce such

[1] I tried once to count these chandeliers, but after reaching 130 had to give up the attempt.

a pretty effect of bright bars over the façade of each large house. The German capital as I saw it last January, illuminated in honour of the Emperor's jubilee, is a sight not soon to be forgotten. All the large public buildings had then put on their diamonds, so to speak. Rivières, or rows of single stones, ran all round each great block, broken at intervals by stars, marguerites, or crosses of larger brilliants. The very gas lamps on the bridges had been conjured, as by the stroke of some enchanter's wand, into imperial crowns, flashing with rubies, sapphires, and emeralds.

"Ja! that *was* a fine sight!" remarked my old *Kutcher*, on that evening, when he had at length extricated his wheels from the dense moving mass of human beings filling every street, and had set me down safely after our slow progress through the chief quarters of Berlin.

During the first days of their married life in Berlin the Prince and Princess Frederick William were occupied in receiving addresses of congratulation from every town and corporation of the kingdom. The public rejoicings took a practical form, also, which was peculiarly congenial to the wishes of the bridal pair. To commemorate the happy event, a number of benevolent associations were founded, such as that which grants a gift of money to poor and deserving young couples on their marriage, quite irrespective of their religious opinions; another which enables the sons of poor farmers to study at the many excellent agricultural colleges in the Fatherland; and a third which provides for widows and orphans. A memorial hall, built at the King's cost during the previous year, had also been decorated by the leading artists of Germany, who now presented their artistic work to the Prince and Princess as a wedding gift.

The palace of the Crown Prince is situated in the Linden Alley, facing the Arsenal, and separated from the Emperor's palace by the Opera House. These royal residences are in friendly proximity to the life of the people of Berlin. The workman as he trudges past to his mid-day meal,[1] looks up at a certain window of the Emperor's palace, where he may often behold the kindly, venerable face of his Kaiser, looking out at him as twelve o'clock brings the "Wache"[2] up the Linden Alley. He generally lingers to chat with his friends gathered round the base of Frederick the Great's statue; and judging by the numbers collected here daily, their Kaiser's countenance is a sight these good fellows do not readily tire of beholding.

[1] Perhaps at one of the fifteen "Volksküchen," or working men's restaurants, which are protected by the Empress. These kitchens afford him a warm and sufficient dinner at a cost varying from 1½d. to 2½d., and *make it answer financially*. [2] Guard.

"In the large family circle which she had entered, the Princess Victoria found many congenial spirits," says Frau Polko: "The Princess Charles, the eldest sister of the Empress, presided over a brilliant circle in those days, and opened her saloons to all who were distinguished in arts and in letters in the capital. She was an accomplished artist, as was her beautiful daughter-in-law, the Princess Frederick Charles.[1] This younger lady was wont also to collect round her the learned and scientific men of the day, of whom the aged Alexander von Humboldt, then in his 90th year, yet still in full possession of his vast intellectual powers, was a distinguished personality." "Such men are the grace and glory of their country—their century," wrote Prince Albert to his daughter, when Humboldt died, a year later. Our Princess is said to have "hung on his utterances" with as much reverence as did her sister-in-law, the Grand Duchess of Baden, in her girlhood.

"This young Princess from over the sea was ever listening, learning, observing, while her small hands were deftly busied either in embroidering after some artistic fashion, or drawing, or modelling. How skilfully she wielded brush and pencil, chisel and mallet, in that quiet studio which exists in each of the royal residences! Her friend, the

[1] The mother of our Duchess of Connaught.

Princess Frederick Charles, might have often been found in those days looking over her shoulder, and watching the artistic creations growing up beneath her clever fingers. . . . Well might the letters, constantly flying home across the wide sea, tell of full and happy days."

The parents, watching so eagerly for every assurance of their daughter's success in her new sphere, were kept, wrote Prince Albert, "Admirably informed. . . The telegraph must have been surprised," he adds, "when it recorded, 'The whole royal family is enchanted with my wife.—F.W.'"

The Prince had once said to his son-in-law, —" You will find that your wife has the heart of a child with a man's head," and to Stockmar he now wrote—" Unquestionably she will turn out a very distinguished woman, one whom Prussia will have cause to bless. . . I write to her every Wednesday by the courier, and receive her answers by the same messenger on the Monday following. We discourse in this manner upon general topics, while she writes to her mother almost daily, giving her the details of her every-day life."

" Should the correspondence between this father and daughter ever be given to the world, what far-reaching wisdom, what sound views on social and political questions it will disclose, if we may judge by the brief extracts scattered through the large

volumes of the 'Life of the Prince Consort.' "—
So said a distinguished English literary woman
recently to the writer.

A shrewd observer in Berlin wrote to her father
a few weeks after the Princess's marriage—" She
sees more clearly, and more correctly, than many
a man of commanding intellect, because, while
possessing an acute mind and the purest heart,
she does not know the meaning of the word
prejudice."

A fortnight after her arrival in Berlin the Prince
Consort wrote to his daughter—" Your exertions
and the demands made upon you have been
immense. . . The public, just because it has
been rapturous, may now grow minutely critical.
. . . This need cause you no uneasiness, for you
have only followed your own natural impulse, and
have made no outward profession which did not
answer to the truth of your inner nature.[1] . .
You will find much to do in studying your new
country, its tendencies, and its people; also in
overlooking your household like a good house-wife,
with punctuality, method, and vigilant care. To
success in the affairs of life apportionment of time
is essential; I hope you will make this your *first*
care, so that you may always have some time over
for the fulfilment of every duty. . . What does

[1] In speaking of Goethe, Max Müller has said, " He was
too great to dissemble."

not pass away, what is alone of value here below, is the old love and constancy of heart and mind; these you will always find awaiting you, come when you may—in truth they have gone with you to your far-off home, and surround you there. . . . If you have succeeded in gaining people's hearts by friendliness, simplicity, courtesy, the secret lay in this—that you were not thinking of yourself. Hold fast by this mystic spell. It is a spark from Heaven."

When the spring had come, and the Court had removed to Potsdam, our Princess found gardening a very pleasant resource. Like her father, she has much taste and talent for horticultural pursuits, as well as for farming and landscape gardening.—" While she delights in flowers, she by no means despises the useful kitchen garden, and in this she resembles the good Queen Louise of sainted memory." One of the gardeners at Babelsberg said to a friend of the writers, speaking of the Princess: " She is head gardener here."

Early in May, 1858, Prince Albert began to think a visit to Germany possible. When proposing a rendezvous at Coburg to the Prince and Princess Frederick William, he wrote—" To see you and Fritz there together in my old home, in a homelike way—I dare not picture it to myself too vividly ! " —At Whitsuntide the Prince was able to set forth

for Coburg; but a bad sprain and consequent derangement of health made it impossible for his daughter to carry out his suggestion and join him there. It was then that her father decided to—
"Make a sudden descent upon the young people, and surprise them at Potsdam."

The Prince was then met at Grossbeeren by his son-in-law, and two happy days were spent at Babelsberg, days which are spoken of in letters to the Queen and to Baron Stockmar as affording him the most complete satisfaction.—"I have been much gratified by my visit here," he says to the latter; "the harmony between the young people is perfect. I am well, and resume my journey this evening, after, alas! a too brief stay. The Prince[1] I found cheerful, but the King is a sad spectacle, and physically much altered."—

In the following August the Queen and Prince Albert paid their first, and, alas! what proved to be their last, visit to their daughter at Babelsberg.—"It beseemed us to do all honour to this great sovereign of a kindred nation, so closely allied to us both by family ties and political sympathies," says Hengst, in allusion to this visit. Although it was intended to be of a private character, the Prince of Prussia met the Queen

[1] Of Prussia. "The Prince's whole aim is to be serviceable to his brother," Prince Albert had previously said, when writing to the Queen.

and Prince at the German frontier, and accompanied them to Potsdam. As the train sped on across the well-cultivated plains of the northern provinces, each substantial town had hung out flags and erected green arches to greet the English Sovereign as she passed. When a halt was made addresses were read.—" At Hamm a broad-headed pastor made us a speech, thanking me for the 'fine present' I had made to Germany in *Vicky*," the Queen's diary relates. At one small station stood " Dearest Lehzen waving her handkerchief," as they went by. The Baroness Lehzen had been governess to the Queen, and furnished the author of the Prince Consort's Life with the following interesting anecdote respecting her young charge. It had been thought advisable to keep the little Princess Victoria in ignorance of her great destiny until she had completed her twelfth year, when her governess left a memorandum in her history book informing her of her claims on the throne. After some explanation and many tears—(" I cried bitterly, and always sincerely regretted this contingency," Her Majesty has recorded)—" the Princess gave me her little hand and said, very solemnly—' I will be good '—again she reached me that little hand, and said—' I will be good.' "—A working man remarked to the present writer lately, " Ma'am, the Queen is a *good lady*, there never was such a monarch as our Queen since the world began!"

The Queen's diary proceeds to relate—"At Magdeburg, Fritz joined us *rayonnant;*" and when, after a long, hot journey, the train stopped at the Wildpark Station—" there stood our darling child with a nosegay in her hand! She stepped in, and long and warm was the embrace, as she clasped me in her arms. So much to say, and to tell, and to ask, yet so unaltered, looking well—quite the old Vicky still! It was a happy moment, for which I thank God. Another five minutes brought us to the Potsdam Station, where were a band and a guard of honour of gigantic guardsmen with pointed caps, and all the Princes and Princesses. . . . Then at the door of the station were the dear Princess (of Prussia) and the Princess Charles (her sister). . . After waiting a few minutes, we got into open carriages, I with the dear Princess and Vicky, and drove up to Babelsberg. The Castle was beautifully lit up. . . My sitting room commands splendid views of the lake, the bridge, Glienicke, the Marmor-Palais, and the Pfingst-Berg, and looks on one of the lovely terraces. . . There are charming walks under trees, and fountains on all the terraces. . . Vicky came and sat with me, I felt as if she were my own again."

The diaries of the Queen, quoted in the " Life of the Prince Consort," give many such delightful pictures of the events of this happy visit.

At its close, Her Majesty relates that the castle and grounds were brilliantly illuminated in honour of the Prince Consort's birthday.—" Round all the walks and flower-beds were placed lamps; wreaths of lamps along the roads; round the fountains brilliant red lights. . . . Glienicke bridge, which had been all lit up by the good kind people of Potsdam, of their own accord, was especially striking. . . And a M. von Bülow played extremely well on the piano in the evening. . . Thus ended this dear day. . . A great happiness to spend it with Vicky and Fritz, the kind Prince and Princess (of Prussia), Fritz and Louise of Baden. . . The last day . . very, very sad."

Amongst the notable persons of whom mention is made by the Queen during her visit to Potsdam, the venerable Humboldt is chiefly remarkable. He had lunched one Sunday alone with the royal party, when the Queen recorded that it was —" Delightful to see such freshness of mind in a man verging on ninety."—Humboldt with his faculties unimpared at eighty-nine; Ranke completing the seventh volume of his "Universal History"—a work commenced when the venerable historian was eighty-five; [1]—when his ninety-second birthday was celebrated last winter in

---

[1] Ranke, alas! has died since these lines were written— "He had such wonderful vitality that he *died hard*," say friends sadly.

Berlin; Moltke still statesmanlike,[1] his clear-cut face serene and beautiful at eighty-six;—these are encouraging examples of the truth of the modern theory, advocated by Mr. Charles Roberts, that full exercise of the mental powers tends to their preservation. It is alleged by him that the brain, if left unused, dwindles and deteriorates, just as a limb must do if tied up. The royal personages whose lives I am endeavouring to sketch, adopt this theory in their practice—a theory of which the German Emperor is himself another and most distinguished illustration.

[1] Witness his vigorous speech of two weeks ago, Dec., 1886.

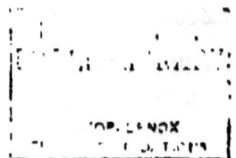

H.R.I.H. PRINCE WILLIAM.

H.R.I.H. PRINCE WILLIAM.

IX.

THE DARKNESS AND THE DAWN.

[1859-1863.]

> *But trust that those we call the dead*
> *Are breathers of an ampler day,*
> *For ever nobler ends.*
> IN MEMORIAM.

KING FREDERICK WILLIAM the Fourth had long been an invalid; his mental powers had begun to fail during the autumn of 1857; there seemed little chance of his recovery; and in the year 1858 his brother, the Prince of Prussia, was asked to assume the Regency. For some years past the King had not been in sympathy with the nation: he had fallen into the hands of a reactionary ministry; and it was felt to be a "blessed hour for the country when the Prince of Prussia became Regent, and the Manteuffel *régime* vanished ingloriously."

"Let me, from my heart of hearts, wish you joy," wrote Prince Albert to the Prince Regent;

"your ministry will command respect both at home and abroad, and you will be applauded for the calm and resolute manner in which you have effected what justice and the best interests of your country seem to demand. . . . Your speech . . . did my heart good, its language was so high-minded, just, and liberal." On November the 8th, the Prince Regent presented his son to his new ministers, of whom Prince Anthony of Hohenzollern was the President.

The year 1859 opened happily for Prussia. Concord reigned between Prince and people, and there was a growing conviction, throughout all the land, that the reins of power were in strong and righteous hands. To add to the feeling of national contentment, an heir (presumptive) to the Hohenzollern throne was born on January the 27th, 1859.

When a telegram announcing the birth of a "fine boy" reached the anxious parents in England, they did not know how grave had previously been the suspense and solicitude in the German capital. When the courier arrived, however, they learnt how anxious, at one time, were the fears for the life of the child.—" Poor Fritz and the Prince and Princess had undergone terrible anxiety," wrote Prince Albert to the King of the Belgians ; " their joy, therefore, over a strong and healthy boy is now all the greater." An aunt of the writer's, then living in Berlin, wrote that the Prince of

Prussia was seen to spring into a cab and drive furiously to his son's residence, during those hours of suspense, before Field Marshal von Wrangel[1] came out on the balcony of the Crown Prince's palace and proclaimed to the crowds waiting below for tidings—"All's well, my children! 'Tis as sturdy a little recruit as heart could wish to see!"

In May, when the Princess paid a short visit to England to be present at the celebration of the Queen's birthday, her parents had the joy of seeing their daughter "blooming, somewhat grown, and in excellent spirits... Dear Vicky is a charming companion," is the entry in her Majesty's diary of this date.

During the spring of 1859 the question of the re-organization of the Prussian army was occupying the Prince Regent and his son very seriously. After the mobilization of the troops a commission was appointed to inquire into the existing state of things, with a view to a reform of the entire military system. The Crown Prince sat on this commission till its close, when he went with the Princess to make holiday in the Tyrol.—"Most heartily do I rejoice in this change for you from the mind-levelling monotony of the sand plains... Look up that lovely passage from the Bride of Messina

[1] "Papa Wrangel," as the Berliners liked to call their veteran general.

—' on the mountains is freedom,' "—writes Prince Albert to his daughter in allusion to this excursion. —He was wont to say that his own best refreshment was to see his "dear Prussian children." After they had paid a flying visit to England, on the occasion of the Prince of Wales's birthday in November, he writes—"Your dear visit has left upon us the most delightful impression; you were well, full of life and freshness, and, withal, matured. I may therefore yield to the feeling, sweetest of all to my heart as your father, that you will be lastingly happy. In this feeling I wait without apprehension for what fate may bring, for that lies in God's hand—not our's."— The Prince had written, shortly before, to the Dowager Duchess of Saxe-Coburg—"Vicky has developed greatly of late, yet has remained quite a child, of such is the kingdom of heaven."

During the spring of 1860 the Crown Princess was much occupied with her chisel and modelling tools. Frequent mention is made of works of art undertaken at this time and sent as gifts by the Princess to her old home. Alluding to a bas-relief of the Two Princes in the Tower, the Prince Consort writes in May—"Your works of art have arrived duly, and, oh wonder! unbroken. I admire them greatly. The composition is charming, and I see the significance of the dog as typifying fidelity, in contrast to the treachery that caused the death of the two innocent boys. Countess Lynar is very like, and makes a pretty medallion." In July—"Your plastic works have arrived... The attitude of Lady Jane Grey is especially natural and happy... They are complete successes." At Christmas—"Your gifts have caused the greatest possible delight, and those we have yet to expect will be looked for with impatience; to the latter belongs Wilhelm's [1] bust."

In June 1860 Prince Louis of Hesse Darmstadt paid a visit to Windsor, when Prince Albert wrote to Baron Stockmar—"There is no doubt but that he and Alice have formed a mutual liking, though fortunately the visit has passed off without any declaration being made."

In July the mother of Prince Louis had written to the Crown Princess confiding to her the great admiration felt by her son for the Princess Alice. The Princess wrote at once to the Queen regarding this communication, and enclosed a portion of a letter from the young Prince himself which was calculated to impress the Queen and Prince favourably.

On the morning after the receipt of this important letter occurs the following entry in the Queen's diary:—"Soon after we had sat down to breakfast came a telegram from Fritz—Vicky had

[1] Eldest son of the Crown Prince and Princess.

got a daughter, and both were very well! What joy! Children jumping about, every one delighted. So thankful and relieved!"

On July the 25th Prince Albert writes to his daughter—"Only two words of hearty joy... The little daughter is a kindly gift from heaven that will, I trust, bring you many happy hours in days to come... I have replied to Fritz on the subject of your late interesting and most important letter, he will impart as much of my letter to you as is good for you under present circumstances. Alice is very grateful for your love and kindness to her... The little girl must be a darling. Little maidens are much prettier than boys. I advise her to model herself after her Aunt Beatrice. That excellent lady has now not a moment to spare. 'I have no time, I must write letters to my niece.' .. The little aunt is too comical. When she tumbles down she calls out, 'She don't like it! she don't like it!' in bewilderment. She came in to breakfast moaning, with tears in her eyes, 'Baby has been so naughty, poor baby so naughty!' . . . What true philosophy!—the child felt it was not *herself* that was naughty."

In September the Prince and Princess Frederick William took their little son to Coburg, where they had the happiness of showing him for the first time to his English grandparents and aunt, the Princess Alice. Prince Albert could seldom revisit the quaint, pretty town of his birth, with its lovely surroundings of wood and hill, and now he rejoiced in the opportunity of showing it for the first time to his eldest daughter.

The palace at Coburg is a noble building, and it is easy for those who have seen it to call up the picture suggested by the Queen's record of a meeting which took place there in September, 1860. The Dowager Duchess of Coburg died, unexpectedly, just as the Queen and Prince had landed at Antwerp. When the royal carriage drove into the inner court of the palace, the Crown Princess and her aunt, the Duchess of Coburg, were waiting to receive them in long pointed veils and deep mourning.—"And then our darling grandson was brought," proceeds the diary. "Such a little love! He came walking in at his nurse's hand, in a little white dress with black bows, and was so good. . . He is a fine, fat child, with a beautiful white, soft, skin, very fine shoulders and limbs, and a very dear face, like Vicky and Fritz, and also Louise of Baden. He has Fritz's eyes and Vicky's mouth, with very fair curling hair."—The royal grandmother again says, "Dear little William came to me, as he does every morning. . . So intelligent and pretty and good and affectionate; such a darling—running about so dearly and merrily."—

The Queen and Prince Consort paused on their

homeward journey, that they might pay a visit to the Prince and Princess of Prussia at Coblentz in company with the Crown Prince and Crown Princess. The scenery of the Rhine had all the charms of novelty for the latter, and while it was enjoyed in company with her parents, whose last happy visit to Germany this was, alas! to prove, the pang of parting was delayed for a few days.

When "the dear Christmas time" came round, the Prince wrote to his daughter, who was then absent from the happy circle at Windsor—"Oh! if you, and Fritz, and the children were only with us!"—Of Prince Louis of Hesse, he says—"In my abstraction I call him 'Fritz'—*Your* Fritz must not take it amiss, for it is only the personation of a beloved, newly-bestowed, full-grown son."

As the year 1861 was dawning, the Prussian Royal Family were gathered at Sans Souci, round the deathbed of King Frederick William the Fourth. In the first hour of the morning of January the 2nd the King was quietly released from his sufferings.—"In seeing the approach of death you have become older in experience than I," wrote Prince Albert to his daughter after this event.

The Prince of Prussia had become King William the First; his son was now Crown Prince, and on the second birthday of the little Prince William, his father received from the King the further title of Stadtholder of Pomerania.

During the following spring the Crown Princess had the grief of losing her grandmother. The death of the Duchess of Kent came with almost overwhelming suddenness upon our Queen, as this devoted mother, in her fortitude and loving consideration for others, had scarcely allowed any one to know how seriously ill she had been for some time previously. Prince Albert saw his eldest daughter and her husband hasten to England to help to sustain the Queen in her bitter grief, with a feeling of grateful relief; this feeling the Prince afterwards expressed in writing to thank the King for facilitating their well-timed visit to England.

In June the Prince and Princess were able to make their English parents a longer visit. When it was over, it was "with heavy hearts"—the Prince records—that they saw them depart, as the time approached for the Coronation of King William at Königsberg. During this visit the Prince Consort had suggested to his daughter, as subjects for her pencil, some passages from the "Idyls of the King," the book which of all others had most charmed him during the past year; perhaps finding there, as its author suggests, "some image of himself."—The Crown Princess was engaged in carrying out these suggestions at the period of her father's death.

On the 18th of October the Crown Prince was stationed betimes outside the gates of Königsberg at the head of a brilliant group of royal and other personages ready to receive the King and Queen. The King rode up, tall and stately, by the side of the carriage, drawn by eight horses, in which sat the Queen, looking—" So handsome, graceful, and distinguished,"—as the Crown Princess in writing to England afterwards described her. The enthusiasm of the populace was boundless, overwhelming; words failed the King.—" He could only hope," he said, " that his son might one day have just such a greeting from them as they were now bestowing on him." The pageant which followed had, as described by Lord Clarendon, a different character from that of 160 years before when Frederick, the first King of Prussia, and his Queen, Sophie Charlotte,[1] were crowned at Königsberg.

King Frederick the First set forth on his journey of 450 miles to Königsberg, "through tangled, shaggy forests, boggy wildernesses, and over many corduroy roads, with eighteen hundred carriages, horsed by 30,000 post-horses."—On that occasion the King's diamond buttons alone cost £1,500 a-piece, but, says Carlyle, with his odd, quaint humour—" The thing that remains for human memories is Queen Sophie Charlotte's very strange conduct on this occasion. She had meditated, from of old, on the 'infinitely little,'

[1] Grandparents of Frederick the Great.

and cared not much about upholstery magnificences. At one stage of the proceedings, the Queen was distinctly seen to smuggle out her snuff-box (being addicted to that rakish practice), and fairly solace herself with a delicate little pinch of snuff. This little pinch is fragrant all along the pages of Prussian history . . inexorable, quiet protest against cant, done with such simplicity."

The coronation of October the 18th, 1861, carried out more, perhaps, in the spirit of Queen Sophie Charlotte, than of King Frederick I., was richer in its proofs of the loyalty, hope, and trust of a whole nation, than any previous royal ceremonial which the ancient kingly town had beheld.

Lord Clarendon writing to the Queen from Königsberg on October the 19th, describes the ceremonial thus—"That most interesting and imposing ceremony took place yesterday, and with the most complete, and unalloyed success. Everything was conducted with the most perfect order—the service not too long, the vocal music enchanting; but the great feature of the ceremony was the manner in which the Princess Royal did homage to the King. Lord Clarendon is at a loss for words to describe to your Majesty the exquisite grace, and the intense emotion, with which her Royal Highness gave effect to her feelings on the occasion."— Many, and older men than Lord Clarendon, who had not his interest in the Princess Royal, were quite as unable as himself to express their emotion at that which was so touching, because so unaffected and sincere.

Lord Granville wrote also at this time from Berlin to Prince Albert—"Every one who has spoken to me agrees that one of the most graceful and touching sights that ever was seen was the Crown Princess's salute of the King." Lord Clarendon, in a subsequent letter, said—"Lord Clarendon has had the honour to hold a very long conversation with her Royal Highness, and has been more than ever astonished at the *statesmanlike* and comprehensive views which she takes of the policy of Prussia, both internal and foreign, and of the duties of a constitutional king. Lord Clarendon is not at all astonished, but very much pleased, to find how thoroughly appreciated and beloved her Royal Highness is by all classes. Every member of the Royal Family has spoken of her to Lord Clarendon in terms of admiration, and through various channels he has had opportunities of learning how strong is the feeling of educated and enlightened people towards her Royal Highness."

The Crown Princess had taken cold at the Coronation festivities, and suffered afterwards from a feverish illness which caused some anxiety to the Queen and Prince Consort during the last weeks of November. The Prince accordingly then entreated his daughter to—"spare herself, nurse herself, and get completely well."—In a letter sent to greet her on her birthday he says—"May your life, which has begun beautifully, expand still further for the good of others, and the contentment of your own mind! True inward happiness is to be sought only in the internal consciousness of effort systematically directed to good and useful ends. Success indeed depends upon the blessing which the Most High sees meet to vouchsafe to our endeavours. May this success not fail you, and may your outward life leave you unhurt by the storms to which the sad heart so often looks forward with a shrinking dread!

"Without the basis of health it is impossible to rear anything stable... Therefore see that you spare yourself now, so that at some future time you may be able to do more. Evermore cherish the determination to exercise unlimited control over yourself, that the moral law may govern, the propensity obey, the end and aim of all true education, as we long ago discovered and reasoned out together."

The Prince Consort had himself been far from well for some weeks previously. It was hoped that he was only suffering from a bad cold; but alarming symptoms began to show themselves with frightful rapidity. It was then that he expressly desired—ever most mindful of those who were dear to him—that his eldest daughter, also far from well, might not be summoned to his sick bed. In obedience to this desire the Crown Princess refrained from hastening to Windsor, and was doomed to never see her beloved father again. It is not needful to speak of the overwhelming grief that fell upon every member of our Royal Family at that dreadful time. Many of us can recall those sad, dark days, when it seemed hard to see how any merciful purpose could underlie so dire a calamity for our Queen and for our native land.

"And yet," said a popular preacher then, "it may be that from this open grave of the Prince such a spirit may rise as shall breathe over the nations a rebuke to human folly, human pride and wrong; that peace, goodwill, and righteousness may now more prevail. . . . He made high places sweet places, he purified the steps of the throne, and knit together the nation into such love for its monarchy as ages past have not seen."

The Crown Prince came to Windsor to sustain the sorrowing family during this time of bitter sorrow. And again, when the sad winter was past, and that second great International Exhibition, which had occupied the thoughts of the Prince

Consort very constantly during the months preceding his death, was about to be held under such strangely saddened conditions, the Crown Prince came, by our Queen's urgent wish, to be present at its inaugural ceremony, in May, 1862. A month later he was once more in London, assisting at the marriage, held very privately, of the Princess Alice with Prince Louis of Hesse Darmstadt.

On the following 14th of August an event occurred which brought new hope and joy to the Crown Princess. Her second son, Prince Henry, was born on that day.

In September of the same year, the King called that great man to be chief of his cabinet who, —" By his bold commanding genius, his masterly statesmanship, was to make the whole German nation great and strong, and to bestow upon it that unity which it had so long desired. Since Luther nailed his Theses on the church door at Wittenberg in 1517 no event of such significance for Germany had occurred as that of September the 24th, 1862, when Otto von Bismarck-Schönhausen became president of the Prussian Chamber."
No sketch of the life of the future German Emperor would be complete without some reference to that great minister who by his statecraft has placed the Hohenzollern dynasty at the head

of a united Germany. Of the political complications of the ensuing years the present writer is not competent to speak. Those who may wish to trace the policy of Prussia during the first difficult years of King William's reign can find it recorded elsewhere. The books of reference already quoted from give a brief outline of those political events, while they speak more in detail of the ever-deepening domestic happiness of the Crown Prince. They inform us also that while he grew more familiar with English thought and English ideas, the Prince was ever teaching his wife to know and love the German Fatherland better.

In the October of 1862 the Prince and Princess, accompanied by the Prince of Wales, set out for a long tour. After cruising in the yacht *Osborne* as far as Tunis and Carthage, and touching also at Malta, where the Princess was able to take some sketches *incognita*, the party landed at Naples, and ascended Vesuvius. Being favoured by very clear weather, the Princess succeeded in getting a sketch on reaching the Hermitage, before proceeding to the top of the mountain on foot. The 21st of November, the birthday of the Princess, was spent in Rome, and on their homeward route the royal party visited Florence, Milan, Venice, and Vienna.

With the thirty-second birthday of the Crown Prince was celebrated, on October 18, 1863, the fiftieth anniversary of the battle of Leipzig—that battle of liberation from which may be said to date the revival of the German nationality. At the close of the military inspection held in Berlin on that occasion, two thousand Knights of the Iron Cross, who had fought on that glorious day fifty years before, and who had come from every corner of Germany to be present and to pass in review before the King and his son, marched past.—" A moving, heart-stirring spectacle!"

Soon after this military display in Berlin King Frederick the Seventh of Denmark died. This was an event fraught with momentous issues for the northern states of Germany. But before proceeding to speak of the three great campaigns of 1864, of 1866, and of 1870–71, let us antedate a peaceful journey undertaken by the Crown Prince in company with Prince Louis of Hesse. When the ceremony of opening the Suez Canal had drawn them so far south as Egypt, it seemed to them then possible to carry out a long-cherished hope and to visit the Holy Land. The Crown Prince travelled to Alexandria by way of Greece, that classic land for which his enthusiasm had so early been kindled. At last he had stood on the Acropolis at Athens; his eyes had rested on the Areopagus where St. Paul had preached of the "Unknown God" to the people ignorantly worshipping Him; but the impression made on the heart and mind of the northern visitor by Jerusalem seems to have exceeded everything that he had hitherto experienced. Herr Hengst quotes many passages from the Prince's diary during his Eastern tour, of which I may translate a characteristic sentence or two.

"This first evening in Jerusalem when I saw the sunset from the Mount of Olives, whilst that sublime stillness crept over the face of Nature which has a solemnizing effect even in less sacred spots, can never, in all my life, be forgotten. Here the spirit, turning away from earthly things, could dwell undisturbed on those thoughts which must move every Christian to the depths of his being—on that retrospect which gives these spots their most solemn and sublime associations. The perusal of some portions of the Gospels in this place is in itself a religious service."

The Prince visited the hospital and school of the Kaiserswerth Deaconnesses while at Jerusalem. He noted at all points of his Eastern journey such beneficent institutions as have been established in those regions by the Germans, and where the young are taught, the sick tended, without any attempt at proselytizing; where those earnest people who are labouring to improve the social and moral condition of their Eastern brethren, try to show them that light which inspires themselves solely by acts of mercy.

Whilst the two German Princes were in the East, the Crown Princess and the Princess Alice had the happiness of spending some weeks together at Cannes. The Princess Alice speaks, in letters to the Queen, with great delight of this visit to a sister she was wont to regard with so much love and admiration. By Christmas time both had returned to their homes in the north. A new year was then dawning, fraught with momentous issues for all the states of the German Fatherland, as well as for the Hohenzollern dynasty.

X.

SEVEN YEARS OF WAR.
[1864-1871].

Arm, arm, my lord; the foe vaunts in the field.
KING RICHARD III.

DR. GEORGE VON BUNSEN has called the first of those three campaigns in which the Crown Prince bore arms—" a war undertaken by Austria and Prussia to protect the ancient rights of the German province of Schleswig-Holstein, in danger of extinction from Denmark in the year 1864."

The Prince assumed no command in that war: he was indeed attached to Field-Marshal von Wrangel's staff, and fought with dauntless bravery in the crowning battle before Düppel, but his mission at the Austrian and Prussian head-quarters was essentially a pacific one. Furnished with ample powers, he arrived at the camp at a critical moment, when disputes had arisen amongst the

Generals in command, and were threatening to bring matters to a dead-lock. A supreme referee was required, and the Prince was chosen to exercise this function. Every question had to come before him for his final decision, and this he pronounced deliberately, unflinchingly, and yet with that fine tact and temper which smoothed away friction, and brought about concord amongst the dissentient commanders.

. He came under fire for the first time before Düppel. In the thick of the battle he was then to be seen cheering on his men to victory, and it was in acknowledgment of "distinguished bravery" that the Order of the Red Eagle was bestowed upon him by the King after that decisive victory. The heroic conduct of his men made a profound impression on the Prince on that day of carnage, when the dark side of even success was painfully borne in upon his heart. On the occasion of the King's last birthday, his son, together with the Crown Princess and von Wrangel, had presented him with a sum of three thousand marks, to found a society in aid of the families of soldiers who had fallen or been disabled in war. On the evening of the battle before Düppel, the Prince dictated an appeal to the country on behalf of this foundation, which was afterwards to be named the "Kronprinzstiftung."

At the Peace of Vienna, in the following October,

the King of Denmark ceded the two Elbe Duchies and Lauenburg to Austria and Prussia respectively. Fifty years after the revival of German independence, Schleswig-Holstein entered the German confederation, "not because of the Bund, but in spite of it," says Hengst.—" A feeling of adhesion to Prussia was now slowly gaining ground, as the royal saying that 'what Prussia gains is gained for Germany,' was beginning to be recognized throughout the land."—In proof of this four States[1] celebrated in the following year, 1865, the fiftieth anniversary of their incorporation by Prussia.

"Only five years previous to the glorious resurrection of the German Empire, the cry had been for the re-establishment of the smaller States of the Empire. Those who then supported Count Bismarck's policy were few, but their number was steadily increasing. . . . With a bold heart and dauntless courage, the great minister pursued his present policy to its glorious consummation, relying on the strength of the national feeling. . . . In the year 1866 Prussia had to prove that while she was entering the lists for her own existence, she was also fighting for the greatest good of the whole Fatherland.

" It was a wise measure to place the approaching

[1] The Rhenish provinces, New Pomerania with Rügen, Westphalia, and part of Saxony.

armament before the German parliament at this time of agitation. Now was the moment to prove who wished well to the people of Germany, who would give them bread, who would give them a stone. . . . The approaching conflict was assuming more and more of a national character, for Prussia's honour and the future of Germany were equally at stake. . . . Prussia went forth against the foe with a mighty energy[1] which astonished the world.—On the 14th of June, 1866, the Bund was dissolved, and a few days afterwards Hanover, Kurhessen, and Saxony were in our hands. The thunderstorm that burst over North Germany was short, and its results were beneficial. . . . The decisive conflict, however, had to be fought between Prussia and Austria. . . ."

Dr. von Bunsen puts the question which was dividing the German-speaking populations into hostile camps in 1866 into a sentence. His account of the situation is this—"A Prussian victory meant the removal of Austria from the German Confederation, with the affairs of which she occupied herself just enough to thwart even the most necessary reforms. Everybody now knows how this result was effected, and that the removal of Austria from the Bund has been the commencement of German unity, and also of a cordial understanding between Vienna and Berlin."—

[1] Gewaltige Thatkraft.

Whilst they were saying at Vienna—"this intermezzo of Frederick the Great must be made to cease," the North was in deep and deadly earnest. On the 17th of June the King called the Crown Prince to the command of the second army corps, further appointing him military governor of Silesia during the mobilization of the army. On the 18th, the anniversary of the battle of Waterloo and of Fehrbellin, the King's manifesto to his people appeared.—"Austria cannot forget that she was once supreme in Germany," said King William; "she sees a rival, not a sister, in our young and rapidly-developing Prussia. . . . The old unholy jealousy has burst into flames; Prussia must be crushed. . . . But in my people the spirit of 1813 is living. . . . If God gives us the victory, we shall be strong enough to renew, in the right and might of the national cause, that loosened bond which has heretofore been holding the Germans together more in name than in reality. God be with us!"

The Crown Prince, addressing his troops from the Silesian head-quarters at Neisse, on the following day, said—"Soldiers of the second army corps! You have heard the words of our King and Commander. The efforts of His Majesty to preserve peace have been vain. With a heavy heart, yet strong in his faith in the gallantry and devotion of his army, the King is now going forth to fight for the honour and independence of Prussia, and for the effective reorganization of Germany . . . ."

On June 19th the third son of the Crown Prince died of meningitis in Berlin. The brief life of Prince Sigismund fell in the interval between the two campaigns. He was born in September, 1864, he died while his father was addressing the troops at Neisse. Of this beautiful boy the Princess Alice wrote in 1865—" Sigismund is the greatest darling I have ever seen, so wonderfully strong and advanced for his age, with such a fine colour, always laughing, so lively that he nearly jumps out of your arms."—

Queen Augusta arrived one day at headquarters to give the Prince the dreadful details of the death of his boy. The young mother was alone in her bitter grief with her dead child, and yet the father never for a moment faltered in his stern duty. Afterwards, when replying to an address of condolence from the citizens of Berlin, the Prince said—" It was a hard trial to be absent then from my wife—my dying boy. Yet, hard as it was, there is at least this much to be said—it was one more sacrifice which I was permitted to make for the Fatherland."—But in the Prince's private journal were written these words—" Ah! victories cannot compensate us for the loss of a child—just the contrary—in the midst of great events, and the greater these events, the more sharply does such a piercing grief wound a father's heart."

Every nerve had now to be strung, for each day brought about momentous issues. On June 26th half the German army, under the command of the Crown Prince, entered Bohemia by the defiles of the Riesengebirge. The corps under the command of Prince Frederick Charles[1] were approaching the scene of action by way of Dresden, in obedience to Moltke's famous rule of marching separately and attacking the enemy conjointly. Four sanguinary battles were fought by the army of the Crown Prince on four successive days. In announcing these brilliant victories, the Prince reported the capture of twenty guns and eight thousand prisoners, with an appalling list of killed and wounded on both sides. The King was now at Gitschin in supreme command of both divisions of the army. A great battle was imminent, and on the night of the 2nd of July a messenger was despatched to the Crown Prince, in hot haste, with orders to immediately join forces with the main army.

The Prince reached the heights above Königgrätz at ten o'clock on the morning of the 3rd.

[1] The "Red Prince," father of the Duchess of Connaught.

A thick pall of smoke hung over the valley, yet after a long look through his glass the Prince could himself discern enough to shew him where he might break in at the *salient angle*, with the most disastrous effect upon the Austrians.—" To him must be due the credit of having grasped this fact. . . . The guards were defiling past a little below where Frederick William stood. See his figure, erect and fair like one of the Norsemen of old, turning towards the soldiers, resolution and self-reliance in every fibre! ' March for that tree;[1] there is our battle-field!'—Every man present felt a thrill when he heard the ringing cheer that followed." — The Prince's movement decided the day.

After the terrible battle had been fought, the victory won, the King and his son were each riding slowly over the battle-field, seeking to succour the wounded and dying, when they met. As they embraced, the King said—" Thou hast shown capacity as a leader."—Bismarck was a spectator of this historic meeting, a fine picture of which adorns the Ruhmeshalle in the Zeughaus at Berlin. The horrors of the field were appalling to the Prince.—" He who causes war with a stroke

[1] Indicating a point about three miles off, where the Prince had seen that a line of Austrian artillery was unsupported by infantry.

of the pen knows not what he is calling up from Hades"—was his entry in his journal on the evening of that momentous day.

That this short and brilliant campaign was brought to so early a close mainly by the prudence and sagacity of Bismarck, is indisputable; but Bismarck has stated emphatically that without the Crown Prince's cool judgment to help him it might then have been impossible to have resisted the counsels of those who were eager to carry war to its bitter end. Of the Prince in relation to this war, Herr von Bunsen says—"It is not enough to praise the modesty which led him to cheerfully submit his judgment to his trusty friend Moltke in the general conduct of the campaign, nor would he do the Prince justice who only commended his courtesy to the common soldier, the merry ring of his voice as he cheers on his men, the true sympathy with which he approaches the sufferers of both contending armies. Such loveable qualities make him the idol of his troops, but would not suffice to inspire that boundless confidence which four years later stood him in such good stead. . . . Let it now be asserted, on the strength of tolerably good information, that the merit of Königgrätz is mainly the Prince's own."

After her defeat at Königgrätz Austria laid down her arms with no loss of German territory; but

Italy once more planted her foot on the shores of the Adriatic.

The victorious armies entered Berlin on the 4th of August. Just four years later, to a day, the Crown Prince was leading his troops to victory at Weissenburg. Of these four intervening years I must not stop to speak at any length, for the supreme event in German history which was then in process of evolution demands more space than can well be given to it within the limits of this brief record. The German Empire was in process of consolidation, while France and Austria were watching the progress of events during those intermediate years with jealous eyes.

The private life of the Prince and Princess was enriched by the birth of their fourth son, Prince Waldemar, in February, 1868. The Princess Victoria, their second daughter, was born just before the outbreak of hostilities in 1866. Although the void left by the death of their third son was still keenly felt, the parents could not but find comfort in the growth and promise of the children still left to them. In January, 1869, Prince William attained his tenth year, when he was invested with the Order of the Black Eagle by his grandfather, as his father had been decorated twenty-eight years previously, by his uncle, the late King. The Princess Sophie Dorothée was born on the 14th of June, 1870, shortly before the great war with France burst forth.

"Why the French should have considered themselves, not the Austrians, vanquished at Königgrätz, no one out of France has ever clearly comprehended," says Bunsen. Whatever may be the opinion of those competent to decide as to the causes of the Franco-German war, there can be no doubt of this fact, that Napoleon was playing into the hand of Germany, in a way he little dreamt of, when, in an evil hour for himself, he challenged the Germans to mortal combat. The very name now given to that war—the War for the German Unity—shows how the Germans regard it.

France had counted on the neutrality, to say the least, of the South German States, while she may have looked for assistance from Austria or Russia. She was dismayed to see the whole of the Fatherland rise like one man, filled with the one inspiring, ardent resolve, to protect the German nationality. Saxons and Bavarians, Würtembergers, Hessians, Badeners, all poured in, to place themselves under the command of the Hohenzollern Prince.—"The attitude of Germany is nothing short of *sublime*"—wrote my aunt from Coblentz in July, 1870. The warm-hearted South Germans were soon enthusiastic in their love for the Crown Prince. They one and all called him "Our Fritz,"—nay, the very French before the end of the war had begun to talk quite *sans gêne* of "*notre Fritz.*"—After the battles of Weissenburg and Wörth had been fought and won, the army of the South was quartered, one soft summer's evening, round a little village in the Vosges.—" The Crown Prince was sauntering alone, pipe in hand, past a barn occupied by a party of Würtemberg troops. Hearing something like stump oratory going on, the Prince opened the door and looked in. Every one rose. " Oh, sit down, I'm sorry to disturb—I dare say there's room for me to do the same," said the Prince, "pray who was making a speech?" All eyes were turned on a sergeant, whose very intelligent countenance, however, looked sorely puzzled when the Commander-in-chief further asked, "And what were you talking about?"—Quickly recovering his presence of mind the sergeant confessed,— " Well, of course we were talking of our victories, and I was just explaining to these young men how, four years ago, *if we had had you to lead us, we should have made short work of those confounded Prussians.*" The Prince roared with laughter, and continued chatting with the party till far into the night."

The events of the war of 1870-71 are fresh in every one's memory, but a few of its incidents may further show what was the personal influence of the future Emperor of Germany during those anxious yet glorious days. He was always at his post, insisting that no account should be taken of his hours of rest, reassuring the citizens and peasants on his march to Paris.—" I claim for the maintenance of my army the surplus of the provisions not wanted for feeding the population," were the words of his general proclamation.—Repeatedly he was thanked by mayors and corporations for the moderation shown to their towns. " It has been said that 'Our Fritz' is the only man not comprehended in that national aversion with which France resents our unsought victories. This is of course an exaggeration; there are Frenchmen noble-minded enough to see both sides of the question . . . but '*notre Fritz*' has been turned in France into a term of good-humoured partiality."

When the army of the Crown Prince halted at Rheims, on its rapid march on Paris, the commandant was proceeding alone to explore that beautiful old cathedral in which, says Bunsen, " so many French kings have been crowned. He was soon so completely hemmed in by the crowd, that he could scarcely move.— 'How is it that this young fellow can go about without attendants?' said the people. 'Why, when Napoleon was here he never stirred out without dozens of gens d'armes and a body of the Cent-Gardes also!'"

One beautiful September evening the third army

corps had gained the heights of Bicêtre. They had had a long march, and a sharp engagement with the enemy. As they lay on the grass the splendid expanse of Paris was visible, spread out beneath them, and lighted up by the rays of the setting sun. A few pitchers of wine were presently brought to them: as they drank, each of these merry South Germans cried, raising his cup, 'To the health of William, German Emperor that is to be!'—When this scene was reported to the Prince, "he felt at the same time elated and sorrowful. The German unity he had so ardently desired to see appeared to be coming, yet not as he had thought it might come, by peaceful treaty or congress—it was coming through fields of bloody carnage and the roar of battle."

On the 18th of October, 1870, the Crown Prince attained his thirty-ninth year. The German troops were then occupying Versailles. At daybreak the "Singverein" greeted him with an *Aubade*, and on his table lay a small pocket pistol and a *necessaire* filled with articles for daily use from the Crown Princess, and a pipe from the Berliners with a portrait of his father painted on the porcelain of its bowl. At night he was again serenaded by the "Singverein," who lulled him to sleep with the strains of Mendelssohn's "Stille Nacht."

The Prince took infinite pains to save the treasures of ancient and modern porcelain at Sèvres when the Commune were shelling it. He was also careful during his residence at Versailles to protect its artistic splendours.

Many a fond wife and mother, far away in the Fatherland, said in those days,—"Ja! my *Mann*[1] is with the Kronprinz, and everybody knows he is well off there. No blind rushing into danger, no needless spending of men's lives is there in the third army corps! Every man is of equal value to *Unser Fritz!*"—Indeed his men were ready to follow him to death with a blind devotion. He never passed down the lines that a thundering "huzzah" did not greet him.—" Of all the thousands then under his leadership," says Hengst, "there was not one who did not bring away the memory of some kindly look or word. The wounded seemed to forget their pain when he was near them. In the hospitals many talked only of him in their last delirium, and seemed to see his image hovering near them as they were dying."

Yet another day—that of the entry of the troops into Berlin—stands out brightly from the records of that long and anxious winter.—By the 7th of March the German army was on its homeward route from Versailles. The Emperor and his son passed through Rouen, Amiens, and Nancy, where

[1] Husband.

they slept for the last time on French soil. They passed by the battle-fields of the previous autumn by Frankfort, Weimar, Magdeburg, and so came back to Berlin. On March 17th the troops made their triumphal entry into the Capital, the Emperor and his son each riding at the head of his own squadron.—" A *splendid man* the Crown Prince looked that day," says an American, who then saw him ride past.—When the Prince had entered his home, crowds, cheering without intermission, filled the whole of the Linden Alley, their eyes fixed on the royal palace. Presently, a window was thrown open, and there stood two tiny creatures, the Princess Victoria, then five years old, and her little brother Waldemar, aged three, waving small pocket handkerchiefs. Behind them were the two young Princes, William and Henry, with the Princess Charlotte, and again behind these appeared the tall, manly figure of the Prince, holding his baby daughter, born just as the war broke out, in his arms. Close beside him was the Crown Princess, all her weary watching and waiting over at last—her treasure restored to her.

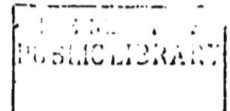

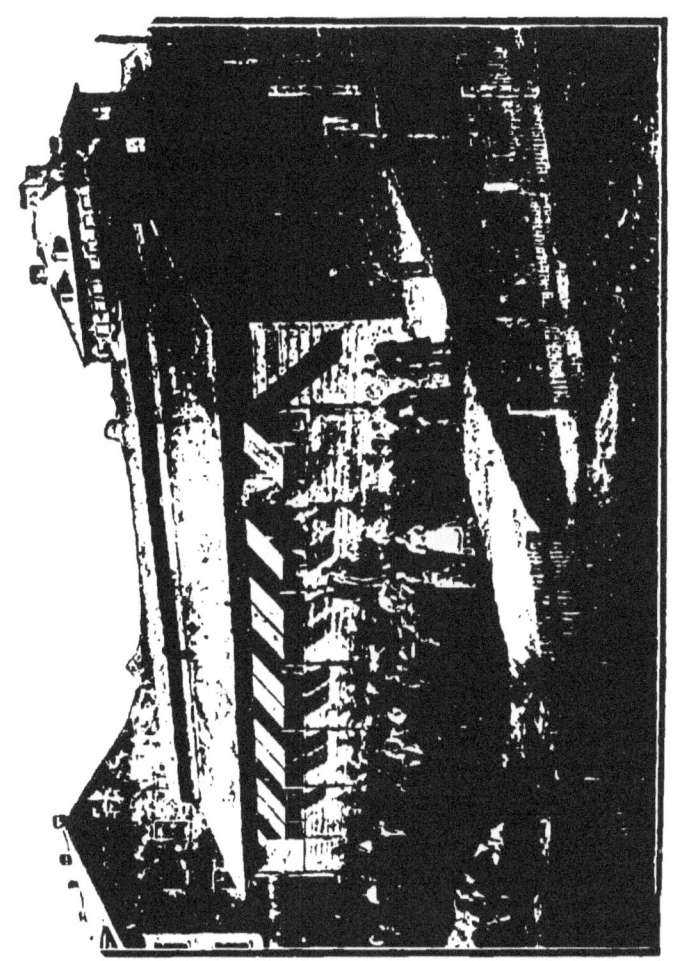

THE VICTORIA BARRACK, HOMBOURG.

XI.

THE WOMEN OF GERMANY DURING THE FRANCO-GERMAN WAR.

[1870-1871.]

> '. . . *Low voices with the ministering hand*
> *Hung round the sick.* . . . *With angel offices,*
> *Like creatures native unto gracious act*
>   . . . *a medium in themselves*
> *To wile the length from languorous hours, and draw*
> *The sting from pain.*
>
> THE PRINCESS.

WE, living safely in our island home, can scarcely realize what the winter of 1870–71 was to the women of Germany. From its royal palace to its poorest cottage, there was no household then that had not sent its best and bravest to defend "mit Gott,"[1] as the Emperor's proclamation ran, hearth and home and native land.—" The heir to the throne, following the noble traditions of his race, had gone forth ready to yield up his life, if need were, for the safety and honour of his country. The Princess, waiting wearily in

[1] With God.

her home, shared the anguish of every German woman during that long autumn and winter. With her clear insight into political complications, she could realize more vividly than those who were less well-informed the frightful contingencies we might have to face. . . . While sympathizing with her countrywomen, she felt also responsible for their support."

Shortly after the outbreak of hostilities, the Crown Princess addressed the following appeal to German people all over the world, on behalf of the families of those who had rallied to the Hohenzollern standard.

"Once more has Germany called her sons to take arms for her most sacred possessions, her honour, and her independence. A foe, whom we have not molested, begrudges us the fruits of our victories, the development of our national industries by our peaceful labour. Insulted and injured in all that is most dear to them, our German people—for they it is who are our army—have grasped their well-tried arms, and have gone forth to protect hearth, and home, and family. For months past, thousands of women and children have been deprived of their bread-winners. We cannot cure the sickness of their hearts, but at least we can try to preserve them from bodily want.

During the last war, which was brought to so speedy, and so fortunate, a conclusion, Germans in every quarter of the globe responded nobly when called upon to prove their love of the Fatherland by helping to relieve the suffering. Let us join hands once more, and prove that we are able and willing to succour the families of those brave men who are ready to sacrifice life and limb for us! Let us give freely, promptly, that the men who are fighting for our sacred rights may go into battle with the comforting assurance that at least the destinies of those who are dearest to them are confided to faithful hands.

"VICTORIA, CROWN PRINCESS."

"And true were the hearts, faithful the hands stretched out in those dark days to succour all who suffered. Our women, led on by the example of the Queen and the Crown Princess, set themselves with practical efficiency to bind up the wounds, to comfort, to relieve. . . . We often now ask ourselves how we could ever have lived through those days, those nights, of deadly anxiety which already seem so far off. . . . The young mother in our royal palace, praying by the cradle of her new-born babe,[1] told her listening children of their father, so far from them, and

[1] The Princess Sophie Dorothee was born shortly before war was proclaimed.

of all the glorious deeds which were done on the soil of France."

The Queen, the Crown Princess, Princess Louis of Hesse Darmstadt, and the Grand Duchess of Baden, often met during that terrible winter, to organise help for the wounded and relief for the sufferers left at home. The touching memoir of the Princess Alice speaks of such meetings, when the Crown Princess was occupying the old palace at Hombourg,[1] so as to be nearer[2] to the battle-fields, and more prompt in succouring the wounded. Queen Augusta had taken the direction of the hospital and ambulance service in Berlin, and under her protection a zealous band of workers, taught by Frau Lina Morgenstern (founder of the working men's restaurants in Berlin), were occupied day and night in the preparation of food for the troops marching daily through Berlin, on their way to join the German armies in France from the Eastern Provinces. Some idea may be gained of what this work involved, when it is known that during the few weeks preceding the first engagement, 59,000 men were supplied at the principal railway stations in

---

[1] This old Schloss was once before the residence of an English Princess. One of the daughters of King George the Third was married to the Grand Duke of Hesse-Hombourg, and lived there for many years.

[2] A telegraph wire connected the castle at Hombourg with the head-quarters.

Berlin with soup, bread, beer, and, if needed, a postcard on which to write to friends at home.[1] There was a more terrible time before these zealous men and women when the prisoners and wounded began to arrive later on. The surprise of the poor Turkos and Zouaves has been described by Frau Morgenstern as touching, when their wounds were so carefully bound up. These wild-looking men, pouring in by hundreds at one time, never, it was said, uttered one rude word, or showed any feeling save one of gratitude to the ladies who tried to ease their sufferings.

The men who were the most severely wounded, however, remained to be treated in the hospitals by the Rhine, while only those best able to bear the long journey were sent on to the Berlin hospitals. All through the Rhenish provinces, the inhabitants were then giving up their houses for the use of the sick and wounded. This was the case with a large house standing near the railway station at Cologne. When talking of the war, its mistress said to me, quite as a matter of course,—"We turned it into a hospital in 1870. We often took in as many as fifty men at once, for it was so conveniently near the station, you see." There were few even of the smaller tradesmen

---

[1] 50,000 post-cards were supplied to the Association for this purpose by Herr Stephan, Postmaster-General.

who did not then open their doors to at least one wounded man, French or German, as it might be.

The ladies who organized the larger hospitals and Field-Lazareths[1] in those dark days, must have had a consciousness of such beneficent usefulness as might go far towards deadening their own anxieties. Foremost amongst these ladies were our own two English Princesses, each carrying on such extensive organizations under her own personal supervision at Hombourg and at Darmstadt respectively. The Princess Alice once wrote to the Queen, when all her four hospitals were full to overflowing,—" I seem to see and smell nothing but wounds."—The Grand Duchess of Baden, whose father, husband, and brother were all commanding in the war, had an excellent ambulance service at Carlsruhe. But of all the hospitals and barracks then in active work, that which had been arranged by the Crown Princess could show the best results, and is, therefore, most worthy of detailed description here.

The Crown Princess had turned the soldiers' barracks at Hombourg into a hospital; the existing hospital[2] attached to the barracks had been re-arranged, and both were thoroughly cleansed,

[1] Field-Lazareth was the name generally given to the newly-erected hospitals for the use of the troops in 1870–71.
[2] This was called the "Militair Hospital," and kept for the use of the wounded French prisoners.

and the best arrangements possible in the limited time, made with regard to ensuring a good supply of water and fresh air. To these two hospitals the Princess added two wards, built in separate pavilions. It was that ward called the "Victoria Barrack" which is said to have shown better results than any other hospital during the war, and which may be described as a model in all respects. The two special wards were used for the more serious cases, and for operations. The four buildings together were named the "Royal Reserve Lazareth," and afforded permanent beds to between 300 and 400 men. Once, after an engagement, 1,000 beds had to be made up.

The Princess herself has said that great results cannot be attained without careful attention to *small things*. The success of the Victoria Barrack was due in some measure to the efficient carrying out of this rule, but its special arrangements also tended to those good results. During the autumn of 1870, the Princess invited Miss Florence Lees, a friend and pupil of Miss Nightingale's,[1] then working before Metz, in charge of the 2nd Field Hospital of the 10th Army Corps, to come to Hombourg in order to superintend the nursing

[1] Miss Lees, now Mrs. Dacre Craven, is honorary inspector of the "Metropolitan and National Nursing Association" for providing nurses for the sick poor, a society founded by herself in the year 1875.

at the Royal Lazareth. At the request of friends, Miss Lees published an interesting account of the nursing work carried on so successfully at Hombourg in *Good Words* for the year 1873. I have permission to quote some portions of her narrative, which give a graphic picture of the times, as well as of the special hospital described.

"The Victoria Barrack, planned by a German architect, received certain improvements at the suggestion of the Princess herself. It was so highly approved by the Americans that a model and photograph of it are preserved at Washington, U.S.A. It was built of wood, on a brick foundation, and contained four rooms, the two smaller of which were used for a store-room and attendants' bedroom respectively. The store-room was provided with glass cupboards for the preservation of lint, linen, etc., from dust, each shelf being properly labelled. Blankets, etc., were laid on high open shelves, while air beds, splints, and such-like were placed on lower shelves.—The best and finest linen for the wounded came from our Queen, who also sent from Balmoral a box of beautifully-knitted woollen socks, to the great astonishment and delight of the soldiers, who told me they thought only *Germans* could knit so well as that.

"From this the ward was reached. It was constructed to hold twenty-four beds, and was

INTERIOR OF THE VICTORIA BARRACK, HOMBOURG.

INTERIOR OF THE VICTORIA BARRACK, HOMBOURG.

well lighted with windows on both sides, and also by small ventilators in the middle of the raised roof. The whole building could be opened from end to end when required, its wooden sides consisting of large "clappen," or shutters, which opened outwardly at pleasure. Small ventilators, to shut or open, were placed near the floor along the whole length of the building. The ward was furnished in the simplest manner, with uncoloured varnished deal furniture, the flooring alone being stained.

"It is almost impossible, however, to describe the bright, pretty appearance of the ward on entering it. There were baskets of trailing plants suspended from the high, open roof; and table-baskets at either end of the room, filled with every variety of flowering plants then in bloom. In the corners stood large evergreen shrubs, and on every table were cut flowers in glasses, occasionally varied by bouquets of hot-house flowers. These had been presented to the Crown Princess, and were immediately sent by her to the Lazareth, with orders that they should be given to the most suffering. . . .

"The bedsteads were of iron, with a horsehair mattress, a bolster of chaff or horsehair, an air-cushion, and good linen sheets and blankets. A water-bed or air-bed was provided for helpless patients. The outer blanket formed the coverlet, and with its broad red stripes folded back at the foot, presented a bright, clean appearance. Each bedstead stood about three feet from the wall, and at its head was a stand for clothes, and a black board, with the patient's name, his injury, and his regiment. At the back were suspended a hand-towel, a warm quilted dressing-gown, and, in cases where the patient could rise and be dressed, such articles of clothing as he might require. Underneath was a glazed calico bag for 'private treasures.' Each patient had also a varnished deal table, with two shelves for combs, glasses, and such like, and a hand-bell, to summon the waiter, a polished tobacco-box, and a small white earthenware ash-pan.

"Nothing was used which would not 'show the dirt.' The crockery was without colour or pattern; the glass unclouded. . . .

"On leaving the ward there was a lobby with a store-room, a smaller division for the convenience of patients, and shelves for basins, foot-warmers, white earthenware pails, sponges, and metal irrigateurs, used in the dressing of wounds and at operations. Two large clothes-baskets, with lids, kept padlocked, held the soiled linen.

"A small kitchen, with a dresser of well-seasoned deal, furnished with plates and dishes; a small gas cooking-stove; and a moveable table which folded back on the wall, disclosing a well-made bath sunk in the floor, and provided with hot and cold water taps, opened off this passage.

"The nursing was done by male and female nurses, trained at Berlin and Darmstadt."

Miss Lees found that one of the great difficulties she had to contend with in managing this hospital was the aversion which all German nurses then entertained to *fresh* air. "I managed, however, to convince them that it was necessary to keep those 'little holes,' which the Princess had made, open. . . .

"Few hospitals were more efficiently visited than this one. The Crown Princess herself attended it daily, never missing a ward, or omitting to speak to each of the patients. . . . I heard a wounded French prisoner describing her visits to his comrades once, after she had left Hombourg.—'Ah, the ladies are all very kind,' he said, 'but none of them are like *Madame la Princesse*. She never passed a bed without some kind word to the unhappy one who lay there; and if she saw that any were more wretched than the others, she talked most to them. Whatever ward she entered, she brought her sunshine with her into it.'"

"Day after day," proceeds Mrs. Craven, "I saw the *Hof-Damen* contriving the best means of aiding these poor men to forget the pain, weariness, and home-sickness, which would at times overpower them. They brought games, puzzles, books, taught them 'Berlin wool-work,' and talked to them of the little 'house-mother' at home, suggesting sometimes that gifts might be made for her.

"A man had one morning received a present from home, of a little square shawl. Man-like, he had tied it tightly round his neck, leaving his shoulders bare. The Princess coming by remarked, —'What a soft, bright-looking shawl you have.'— 'It *is* very pretty, Royal Highness, but it has a fault; it is a trifle too small—my shoulders are so broad it won't cover them,' and he gave a tug to right and left to show how hopeless it was. 'We will see if it cannot be arranged,' said the Princess. She took it off, folded it shawl-wise, and pinned it round him, to his great delight and surprise.

"I noticed one day, when making my rounds, that a man named Pfeffer, well enough to be up, had thrown himself on his bed again, and was shaking with suppressed sobs. . . . 'Are you in great pain?' I said—'Ach! no, it is not that; I have had bad news from home,' he said,—' My boy! my little one I have never seen!—I never shall see him now,' the poor fellow added, and then he told me that he had only been married a year when he bade his wife farewell—that very day their boy was born. Since then, all the letters had been filled with descriptions of the little one.

Often had he thanked God for sending such a comfort to one he had left in such sorrow. When he was wounded and sent back, how he had thought of her coming, and bringing their first-born with her! This very day the poor little 'house-mother' was coming—*alone*—the boy was dead! While I was trying to comfort him, I heard that Pfeffer's wife was waiting outside. Before the door stood one of the prettiest women I had seen in Hesse, in her short skirt and tightly-fitting bodice; but her eyes were dim with weeping and watching. I arranged that she should see her husband in my room, and then I went up to the Schloss. When her Royal Highness heard the story, she expressed the warmest sympathy with the young people, and desired that they might be sent to the castle when the little 'house-mother' next came, and this was done—but I must describe the interview in the words of the little wife herself.—' The Frau Kronprinzessin came to us, and said that she had heard of our great sorrow, and was *grieved;* and then she said—ah! such beautiful words about the happiness which the good God had given us by sparing us to each other, and of the happiness which the *future* might bring us. And when she left the room, it seemed as if our trouble was easier to bear. It was like sunshine after the storm; and my husband and I both felt that God had indeed been very good to us.' "—This little story brings both the sweet and the bitter side of those anxious days before us.

I spent the autumn of 1870 in the companionship of an English friend whose brother was fighting with the Würtemberg troops, and had been in the heat of the two great battles of Wörth and Weissenburg. The first pencilled lines written on a drum-head, in all the smoke and roar of battle, to tell the anxious sister of his safety, reached us when we were in the heart of the Highlands. The great, silent hills all round about Braemar would send down their shepherds and gillies every evening to learn the news, when that often belated mail-coach used to come in with letters and papers. The Highlanders then gathered round the post-office, while the fortunate possessor of an Aberdeen paper read the war news aloud for the benefit of all in the clear September twilight of those northern regions. We were surprised to find how intelligently and eagerly these men, so quiet in manner, so slow of speech, seemed to follow the course of the campaign, and to notice their keen interest in the movements of the great armies. They knew, it is true, that the husbands of two of the Queen's daughters—those kind young Princesses who long ago were wont to come in and out of their cottages—were in the thick of that turmoil of battle, commanding the vast armed forces then fighting on French soil.

One evening a gillie came speeding up the glen from Balmoral, bringing the exciting news that Sedan had fallen—Napoleon had capitulated—news just flashed to the Queen from head-quarters. For many nights past there had been beautiful displays of the Aurora Borealis, but that evening the Northern Lights were more striking than on any previous occasion. As the fiery lances seemed to dart from horizon to zenith, our thoughts took wing and bore us to those far-off fields of France, where the Würtemberg troops, led by the Crown Prince to victory, were often in such deadly peril, and were winning laurels both for their bravery and for their forbearance.—Our Queen, too, was watching here, in the remote Highlands, with an anxious heart, for tidings from the seat of war.

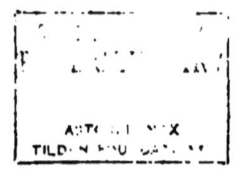

H.R.I.H PRINCESS WILLIAM.

XII.

SEVEN YEARS OF PEACE.

[1871-1878.]

> "*On the good education of princes, especially of those who are destined to rule, the welfare of the world in these days very largely depends.*"
> **THE PRINCE CONSORT.**

THE winter of 1870-71, with its wearing anxieties and ceaseless work, was followed by a period of tranquil domestic happiness for Germany, and for Germany's future Emperor and Empress.

In the spring of 1871 they visited England. In July, the Prince was received at Munich with great rejoicing. "Your Imperial Highness has gained the love of our Bavarian troops, and of our Bavarian people," said the Burgomaster, when he met the Prince at the gates of the city, "Henceforth, there can be no discord between the North and the South." During the autumn months the Crown Prince had many such greetings from the principal German towns.—" Young girls frequently came out to present him with laurel wreaths as he approached, and the assurances of fidelity which were showered upon the Hohenzollern Prince were universal as they were enthusiastic and sincere."

In April, 1872, the Princess Margaret, the youngest child of the Prince and Princess, was born. Her christening gave occasion for a charming Garden Fête at the Neue Palais in the month of June. People who were then present describe the scene as one of almost magical beauty, while they say that, like all the entertainments given by these royal hosts, it was characterised by a delightful unconstraint. The aristocracies of birth and talent, of art and learning, were all represented amongst the guests then entertained. In the November of this year the Crown Prince was seized, while visiting his sister at Carlsruhe, with a sudden and alarming attack of illness. In consequence of this seizure the Prince, with the Princess and his family, spent the winter months at Wiesbaden, returning to Berlin in March.

The education of their children has been regarded by these royal parents as the most vital concern of their lives. It was their custom to visit their nurseries and schoolrooms together, each morning, the Princess repeating her visits frequently in the course of the day. A lively interchange of thoughts and ideas was maintained with both pupils and teachers, while their mother even might have been found occasionally joining in the lessons of her sons and daughters. Both parents were invariably present when the examinations took place at the end of each term.—" The Princess in her nurseries, used to be the theme of every tongue. This excellent mother thought no detail, however trivial, unimportant, which could tend towards the physical and moral health of those who may one day be called to fill responsible positions. Her sons were taught to become self-reliant, simple in their tastes, and considerate for all who came into relation with them. Her daughters saw their mother occupied in purely womanly ways. A spinning wheel stands in the Princess's room, that room where so many small garments have been shaped, and sewn, and embroidered by her own clever hands for her little ones." — Warmth of heart, which, when combined with strength of will, is the foundation of so many manly virtues, has always been encouraged in this royal household.

As the day might often bring unavoidable distractions, the boys' lessons began invariably at six o'clock in the summer and at seven in the winter months. By half-past nine, the breakfast hour, the most difficult and important tasks had usually been accomplished. At eleven, work was resumed for two hours. At one, came another interval of two hours, and in the course of the afternoon the tasks for the following day were prepared. When the time approached for Prince William's confirmation, his parents occupied themselves anxiously in the choice of a religious instructor who might be likely to impart a living faith to their son, rather than the dry bones of a merely formal creed.—" Dr. Perseus, a man of enlarged views, was invited to state to them his opinions in writing, and, after a careful perusal of these statements, the Prince and Princess confided this important trust to him, a trust which was fulfilled so entirely to their satisfaction as to obtain an expression of their warm thanks afterwards."

To Dr. Hinzpeter—" of whose wisdom and conscientiousness it would be difficult to say too much " — was entrusted the general education of Prince William and his brother. In relation to this gentleman, Dr. von Bunsen relates the following anecdote.

"One day Prince William appeared in the school-room deeply mortified by something which had occurred. He related the circumstances, and asked, with tears, whether his father had not wronged him. The dilemma was somewhat awkward. Dr. Hinzpeter, after considering a moment, said—' I think your father has done you wrong, if so, he will be sorry.'—With this, after setting his pupil to work, he left the room, but returned soon with a summons to the Crown Prince. Tremblingly did the son walk in, to come away soon with a beaming face. When they left, the father took Dr. Hinzpeter's hand into his own, thanking him with the words—'I trust that you will preserve to us your uprightness and truth.' ".

When Prince William had attained his fifteenth, Prince Henry his twelfth, year, their parents came to the high-minded resolution of parting from them, and allowing them to enter one of the great public schools of Germany.—"A magnanimous resolve, heretofore unexampled in the annals of our reigning families."

One September morning, in the year 1874, the Crown Princess arrived by an early train at Cassel, a clean and handsome town which can boast of possessing one of the best Latin Grammar Schools in Germany. In the course of the afternoon she was joined by the Crown Prince, who had been attending the autumn manœuvres at Friedeberg. In the evening these parents paid a visit to the Head Master, Dr. Heussner, in order to arrange with him about the education of their sons. Prince William entered the fifth form, Prince Henry, for the present, was to have private tuition, both Princes residing with Dr. Hinzpeter, who accompanied them to Cassel.—"There was no ceremony, no etiquette, only the utmost friendliness in the dealings of these royal parents with the school authorities. By their express desire, Prince William was treated just in the same way as the other pupils. He was addressed as "you," and answered to the name of "Prince William." He associated with the other boys, in play and in work, quite *sans gêne*, and came up for examination at the end of each term with all the rest.—" During those days the grandson of the Emperor, himself the heir presumptive to the imperial crown, might have been seen trudging to school with his book of logarithms under his arm. He was never excused his Livy or his Homer, his trigonometry or his history, and worked with an industry and zeal which ensured his success. When the final examinations came the Prince passed with distinction."—The correspondent of an English newspaper reported in those days that—"no one, to see those two simple, kindly looking lads in their plain military frocks, sitting on a form at the Cassel Gymnasium amongst the other pupils, would have guessed that they were the two young Imperial Princes."

Shortly after her marriage King William had presented his daughter-in-law with the estate and farm-house of Bornstedt, close to the Neue Palais at Potsdam. Here the Crown Prince rears his prize animals, the Princess has her model dairy, and here, emulating the ways of the "good farmers" of Osborne of an older generation, they come into contact with the kindly tillers of the soil. Here, it was, that the Princess once arranged for her two eldest sons to reside during the Christmas holidays.—" It is well," said this excellent mother, "for young people to accustom themselves to simple ways."—Their parents were spending Christmas with our Queen. One morning a letter from England came to the two young Princes. —" Have you remembered," it said, " who you are, and what it is incumbent upon you to do at this season? We, your parents, are far away from our dear sons, from our home. You, our children, must be our representatives. Seek out the poor, the suffering, in the cottages around you, and give to them freely, according to your means."—All who come into association with the two young Princes speak of their kind consideration for others, of their sympathetic interest in those who are in attendance upon them, as well as of the great charm of manner by which they are distinguished.

On January 27th, 1877, Prince William completed his eighteenth year, and was, according to the royal law, of age. He then quitted Cassel and entered his father's old regiment, the First Foot Guards, in order to study the practical work of an officer before entering the University at Bonn at the approaching October term. Prince Henry quitted the Gymnasium at the same time, to be received into the navy. In March he was confirmed, together with his eldest sister, the Princess Charlotte. Confirmation is a still more important event in the lives of the young in Germany than here. Four days later the Emperor publicly announced the betrothal of his young granddaughter to Prince Bernard of Saxe-Meiningen.

When Prince Henry joined the ship *Niobe*, as a midshipman, his parents accompanied him to Kiel, and saw him established in his new sphere. The chief of the Admiralty department, General von Stosch, addressed the following words to the Prince and Princess on that occasion.—" His Royal Highness Prince Henry, is the first member of our Imperial House who has preferred the navy to the army. This is a pleasant proof to us that our exalted military commandant is disposed to place the naval on the same footing as the military service."

While the older members of the Royal Family were approaching maturity, the younger children were as yet enjoying the golden days of their happy youth. Each spring brought them back their own little kingdom of pretty gardens and bowers, when they returned with their parents to the Neue Palais, at Potsdam. The summer residence of the Crown Prince and Princess was built by Frederick the Great, to show, it was said, that there was still some money left in the exchequer after his military campaigns were ended. Surmounting this grand structure, built in the *rococo* style of architecture, is a royal crown, held aloft by three slightly-draped ladies supposed to be the three graces, but bearing—say those who look at them critically—an amusing resemblance to those three female potentates who had laboured the most to thwart the great Frederick's purposes—Maria Theresa, Empress of Austria; Catherine, Empress of Russia; and Madame de Pompadour, all-powerful in France in the days of Louis XV.

The little gardens of the royal children are in close proximity to the green *coulisses* of the *al fresco* theatre designed by the great Frederick. Little flower-beds and yellow-pebbled walks are here disposed round a pretty fountain, while a summer-house stands conveniently near for shelter from showers. Close by are to be found miniature earthworks and fortifications, and a cricket field, the scene of much mirth, when those school children, who are so kindly entertained, from time to time, by royal hosts, have gathered here from the neighbouring villages, or from Berlin.

"One fine June morning," relates Herr Hengst, "a special train brought a crowd of little scholars from Berlin to Potsdam. Presently a second band of children arrived, marching to the strains of the

Bornstedt band, and joined forces with the others in the grounds of the Neue Palais. Then came the Crown Prince and Princess, with their sons and daughters, to give kind words of greeting and welcome to all these little people.

"Soon the young Princes and Princesses were busied in starting games and arranging prizes for their little guests. Fine dragons, trumpets, popguns, purses, gloves, braces, swung temptingly aloft from the tops of poles and climbing ladders. The Princes showed the boys how they might climb and possess themselves of these treasures. The Princesses placed such little articles as are dear to every small maiden's heart on low stands, set in a circle, and were meanwhile encouraging the little girls, who stood with bandaged eyes in the centre of this magic ring, to aim well so as to win prizes. Two long tables stood near, heaped with every species of good German cake, while great cans of fragrant coffee and steaming milk lurked beneath the branches of the great trees hard by.

"Presently the Crown Princess might have been observed to cast a critical eye over these tables, when, having assured herself that all was in readiness, the hungry little people were invited to approach. They seated themselves to the sound of music, and after a short but fervent grace had been said by the Bornstedt pastor, were soon enjoying the good things prepared for them, their young hosts and hostesses going round to see that all were well supplied, when, suddenly, some big drops of rain were felt, and before long a veritable deluge was descending! Everybody ran to the trees for shelter, but soon the rain had penetrated through the thick leaves, and little Sunday frocks began to feel sadly limp. Then came the Crown Prince himself, and gathered all these little dripping people together and led them into that famous grotto saloon—filled so often during a former century with splendid ladies and gentlemen. A great fire of logs was soon crackling in the wide fireplace, and as many as could come near enough to get dried were gathered close round the cheerful blaze. The rest of the damp little company were set to jump and march about briskly to the sound of music, that they might not get chilled. Songs were sung in chorus, poems recited, a little fable was acted, and all the while their kind hosts never relaxed their personal care that colds might not be caught, and that the enjoyment of the day should not be marred."

"No children have enjoyed the privilege of making others happy more frequently than the sons and daughters of our Imperial Prince and Princess. How rich and happy too their own childhood has been! In former days a little cavalcade, mounted on ponies, might often have been met in the royal parks, while the air was filled with silvery laughter,—father and mother watching their little ones as they cantered past, with happy eyes. That charming trio, the daughters of Prince Frederick Charles, and their brother, who was three years older than the bright little Waldemar—the universal favourite—were the constant companions of the Imperial Princes and Princesses in their childish sports."

The happy years sped on, the Crown Prince renewing his own youth in his sons, the Crown Princess watching her eldest daughter blossoming into womanhood, till, at length, one morning the sound of wedding bells was heard, and the old Schloss in Berlin was decked with flowers and garlands in honour of two happy brides.

On the 18th of February, 1878, the Princess Charlotte of Prussia was married to the hereditary Prince of Saxe-Meiningen, while at the same time, and at the same altar, her cousin, the Princess Elizabeth, was joined in wedlock to the hereditary Grand Duke of Oldenburg. The Empress placed the bridal crown on each fair young head as it was bent before her. The court chaplain wove into his address the respective mottoes of the two bridegrooms, the "Treu und fest"[1] of Meiningen,

---

[1] "True and steadfast."

the "Ein Gott, ein Recht, eine Wahrheit,"[1] of Oldenburg. Amongst the guests then present were the King and Queen of the Belgians, and the Prince of Wales. The brides are both very lovely, and the wedding was described at the time as presenting a beautiful touching spectacle.

[1] "One God, one Right, one Truth."

T.R.I.H. PRINCE WILLIAM, PRINCE FREDERICK, AND
PRINCE ADALBERT.

T.R.I.H. PRINCE WILLIAM, PRINCE FREDERICK, AND PRINCE ADALBERT.

XIII.

GRIEF AND JOY IN THE HOME.

[1878-1886.]

> *"Though weeping may endure for a night, joy cometh in the morning."*
> PSALM XXX.

WHILE the Crown Prince and Princess were in England, during the spring of 1878, alarming news reached them from Berlin. A shot had been fired at the Emperor when he was driving, with the Grand Duchess of Baden, in the Linden Alley. The assassin, however, had missed his aim, the people of Berlin were proving their loyalty, and their abhorrence of crime by public rejoicings and illuminations, and all was, apparently, well. The German workmen of London, desirous of also showing their joy at the safety of their venerable Kaiser, had organized a loyal national demonstration, but violent proceedings of certain restless political refugees threatening to disturb the public peace, they were advised to present their address of congratulation to the Crown Prince and Princess privately, at the German Embassy. A deputation, consisting of fifty tradesmen, was accordingly received there with much friendliness. The Prince shook hands with each of the men, while the Princess inquired to what schools their children went, and whether they could sing the little songs of their native land. To a carpenter the Prince remarked, "I am a carpenter too." Each man had a special word from his Prince, and all came away delighted.

A few days later, a second and, as it proved, a more disastrous attempt, was made on the life of the aged Emperor. Filled with horror and alarm, his children hastened to Berlin to find their father severely wounded, and in much suffering. The papers of the day tell of the courage and patience with which the Emperor bore his long subsequent illness, as well as of his anxiety that the man who had wounded him should be spared the utmost penalty of the law. They told that when his daughter rushed to his bedside, after the dreadful event, her father's greeting to her was—"It was well thou wert not with me this time!"—Two tender and devoted nurses, the Grand Duchess of Baden and the Crown Princess, smoothed his pillow, and tended him at this trying period, with untiring love. It was by the "soft persuasive prayers" of the latter lady that at last he was persuaded to exchange his hard camp bed for an easier couch.

As the Emperor was unable to attend to affairs of state, he desired that his son should carry on the government of the country in conjunction with Prince Bismarck, the Chancellor of the Empire, during the many months of his illness.

Sorrows too often tread fast on one another. Before this sad year was ended another great grief had fallen on our Princess and her husband. Her sister, the gentle and devoted Princess Alice, passed to her eternal rest on December 14, 1878, the fatal day on which, just seventeen years previously, she had hung over the death-bed of her beloved father. During the winter of the great war the Princess Alice had suffered frightful anxieties; she had spent her strength over-much for the relief of the sick and wounded; her lovely boy, that little "Frittie," named after the Crown Prince, had been killed by an accident before her very eyes; another sweet child, the little May—her mother's "May Sunshine"—had died of diphtheria; and when the Princess was herself seized with the same deadly complaint, it was impossible for her exhausted powers to resist it.

This was not the only bitter sorrow which the Crown Prince and Princess were called to endure in the course of that dark winter of 1878-9. In March their youngest boy, that most promising, most beautiful Waldemar, of whom his tutor said—"He was the brightest of God's creatures,"—died of that frightful complaint diphtheria, which had been so fatal at Darmstadt a few months previously. The grief which then fell upon the hearts and lives of the royal family is too sacred to be intruded upon here.

Yet comfort was not far off, that consolation which an unconscious little child may bring when all other sources of earthly relief fail. In May, 1879, the young Princess of Meiningen became a mother. Her lovely little girl—the first grandchild of the Prince and Princess, the great-grandchild of our Queen,[1] as well as of the Emperor William—came just when the hearts of the sorrowing family most needed her sweet ministrations.

In June, 1879, the Emperor and Empress celebrated their golden wedding. "In the Rosenmond"—the moon of roses—says Herr Hengst, "this young pair were united, and now, just fifty years after the Princess Augusta, then only eighteen years old, had quitted Weimar, the home of the muses, as the wife of our true-hearted, wise, and invincible Prince William, the golden rose bloomed, and the love of a free and loyal people was enriching the happy anniversary."

[1] A great-grandmother at sixty.

As the winter approached, it was thought advisable for the Crown Princess to seek a more southern climate, and she went, with her children, to reside for some months at Pegli, near Genoa. Here, the loveliness of nature, the soft air and Italian sunshine, with the abundance of subjects offered to her pencil and brush by the scenery of the Riviera, proved healing alike to the spirit and to the bodily health.

A large and fine landscape, painted by the Princess while at Pegli, was engraved in the *Magazine of Art* for May, 1886. The critic who then contributed an article on the work of "A Royal Artist" to this Magazine speaks of the many directions in which that artist's talents are exercised. Alluding to this drawing, he says—"There is an air of sincerity about it which proves that the Crown Princess goes straight to nature for her subjects. . . . Her work is far above the standard of most amateurs."

In May, 1880, the Princess visited Rome and Naples. Her interest was much stirred by the large schools established by Mrs. Salis Schwabe for the training of pauper children in the latter place. These institutions include a Kindergarten, a school for older boys and girls, a training college and boarding-house for Kindergarten teachers, and a school of art. Immediately after her arrival in Naples the Princess visited these establishments.

—" The little black-eyed children at the Kindergarten greeted her by singing the German National Hymn in Italian, to the tune of our " God Save the Queen." Then the smallest child brought her a bunch of flowers, and when he broke down in his speech the Princess helped him; she kissed him, and taking a pansy out of the bouquet, gave it to him, to keep in remembrance of her. She then proceeded to examine all the arrangements of the house with great interest. When the mid-day meal was served she ate some spoonfuls of the soup, and praised it. She entered into the smallest details of the management of all four institutions, and made herself thoroughly conversant with the principles on which they are worked. The Princess visited Mrs. Schwabe again during the evening, remaining for some time to discuss the subjects which are so interesting to her."

The Crown Prince was able to be with his family frequently during the winter of 1879-80, but many duties called for his presence in Germany during the following summer. On the 1st of May he opened an Exhibition of Arts and Industries at Düsseldorf, which has left, as a legacy to that cheerful, prosperous Rhine town, a good permanent museum, admirably arranged, as are all German museums. Carlyle has it that—" genius consists in an infinite capacity for taking pains." Our

Teutonic brethren can surely bear the palm from all European nations in respect of painstaking.

It was at this time that the Prince visited the interesting institution, founded fifty years ago by Pastor Fliedner at Kaiserswerth, near Düsseldorf. Originating though it did in the sheltering of one discharged female prisoner in the summer-house of his garden, Pastor Fliedner was able before he died, to see his noble work spreading to all quarters of the globe, and to count his Protestant Deaconesses' Homes, Hospitals, Schools, and Refuges, by the score. When we visited the large parent institution by the Rhine last June, the kind sisters spoke of their genial Crown Prince as recalling, on the occasion of his visit to Kaiserswerth in 1880, his visit to their schools in Jerusalem eleven years previously. Of this he was reminded when he saw the collection of articles which had been sent to the " Mother House "[1] from its affiliated branches all over the world.

A Fisheries Exhibition, which proved very beneficial to the seaports of Germany, claimed the attention and assistance of the Prince in Berlin during the same month. He visited an Exhibition of Arms, at Cleves, shortly afterwards. In June, 1880, Prince William, who had completed his twenty-first year in the previous January, was betrothed to the Princess Victoria of Schleswig-Holstein. The family party in celebration of this

[1] So the Kaiserswerth institution itself is always called.

happy event took place at Babelsberg, and has been described as especially interesting.

In August the Prince and Princess were present when the Old Museum in Berlin held its jubilee. The Prince, in his presidential address, alluded to those dark days in the nation's history when this great means of culture for the people was first called into existence by patriotic Germans. He then went on to remind his hearers that—" while enjoying these results of the noble efforts and designs of our ancestors in our own happier days, we can only do so truly and honestly when we acknowledge the responsibilities they involve, and share the enjoyment of our treasures with our fellowmen. . . . This place, devoted to the preservation of the highest creations of human genius, exists for the benefit of the men and women of our whole nation "—said the Prince in conclusion.

A month later, the completion of the Cologne Cathedral gave occasion for rejoicings all over Germany. The Emperor assisted at the solemn and impressive Roman Catholic service which was held in the morning; the Crown Prince made a striking speech at the banquet which concluded the ceremonies.—" This great building," said the Prince, " was commenced at a brilliant period of our national history. The people of Germany have experienced many vicissitudes of fortune in those long centuries during which it has been in process of completion. To our own generation it is at length granted to see it fully perfected. May the history of this great monument of German unanimity encourage us to hold fast by our best national possessions—our German character and modes of thought, our God-fearing piety, our earnestness and sincerity in work, in research, in the pursuit of art and science. The whole nation has combined to produce this building, this symbol of our fidelity and our unity. May it endure, a great monument reared for the delight of unborn generations by a happy, a united, and a peace-loving Germany."

Just before the Christmas of 1880, Prince Henry returned from his two years' cruise round the world, when his parents went to meet him at Kiel. This was a sad, as well as a happy meeting, for he had been far away on the high seas when his brother died. A few weeks later the young bride made her public entry into the capital, and Prince William led her to the altar in the Chapel Royal of the Old Palace, on the 27th of January. The accounts of this magnificent ceremonial have appeared in our papers so recently that it is scarcely needful to enlarge upon it here. The Crown Prince is reported to have said that no one could measure the blessing that came into the Imperial family with this amiable and gentle young lady. Prince William, say persons who are frequently brought into contact with him, possesses in a peculiar degree that kind and considerate disposition and manner which he inherits from both the royal houses from which he is descended. Of both the young Imperial Princes it is constantly said in Berlin—" They are clever, and *perfectly charming*."

The public rejoicings for this marriage were scarcely over, when all Europe stood aghast at the horrible murder of the Czar Alexander of Russia. The Crown Prince at once announced his intention of attending the funeral. There were anxious hearts in England, as well as in Germany, until the representatives of many great dynasties then collected at Moscow were announced as having safely returned from their painful mission. Many persons tried to dissuade the Crown Prince from venturing on this journey; but it was undertaken without a moment's hesitation, and with—" that courage which a strong character feels in the accomplishment of a great duty."

Early in June the Empress was seized with an alarming illness; but by the skill of her medical advisers she had sufficiently recovered by the end of the month to enable her son to leave her and proceed to England.

On the 18th of October, 1881, the Prince completed his fiftieth year.—" It is his modest custom to decline all public recognition of this day, but on that occasion ' Our Fritz' could not avoid receiving the honest expression of a whole nation's love which the newspapers brought him."

"One fine May evening in the year 1882, the Crown Prince might have been seen, pacing up and down, with a grave and anxious expression of countenance, beneath the windows of the Marmor Palais at Potsdam, the residence of Prince William. The Crown Princess had been with her young daughter-in-law for some hours previously. Suddenly a window was thrown open, a pale and agitated face looked out.—" Papa ! " cried an unsteady voice, " Papa ! it is a boy ! " —" The private lives of Princes are supposed to be guarded from the public ken by a screen of reserve, and yet that screen is sometimes transparent. Our Princes belong to their people even as parents belong to their children, and well is it for any nation when the domestic lives of its Rulers can present such a picture as this."

When the Emperor held his great grandson in his arms, on the following day, the grandfather and father standing by, it was said—" Here are four Emperors under one roof."—The little " Frederick William Victor Augustus Ernest" was christened on the fifty-third anniversary of the marriage of the Emperor and Empress. Two little brothers have come to him since then. The three baby faces smile at you out of a " Kleeblatt," or trefoil frame, which stands on their great-grand-father's writing table at Babelsberg. Two other great-grandchildren of the Emperor's—little Swedish Princes—are to be seen there also, together with a life-size portrait of the Empress, and other interesting family photographs. A double festival was held at Carlsruhe in the autumn of 1881, when, on the silver wedding-day of the Grand Duke and Duchess of Baden, their only daughter, the Princess Victoria, was married to the Crown Prince of Sweden.

Another silver wedding was approaching. On January the 25th, 1883, Dr. G. von Bunsen writes to the people of the New World—" Berlin is instinct with simple, unostentatious sympathy. Everything has been done so as to give the most pleasure to the Crown Prince and Crown Princess. This city has voted a sum to be placed at their disposal for training nurses for the sick poor; a larger sum has been silently collected throughout Germany, to be utilised for any charitable institutions they may wish to assist. . . . Several cities have combined to furnish their dining hall afresh. A loan collection of pictures, in the possession of private owners, has been opened expressly for the occasion. The Berliner walks about, perfectly contented, in the bright sunshine of a frosty day in January.—Frederick William and Victoria his wife, with their children, are at church."

Amongst the gifts presented to the Princess on that day was a collection of photographic groups of the little children at work in the Pestalozzi-Fröbel House, which claims the warm sympathy and interest of her Imperial Highness. Some specimens of these groups will illustrate a later chapter.

I chanced to be passing through the German capital when the twenty-fifth anniversary of the Emperor's accession to the throne of Prussia was celebrated in 1886. Sunday morning, the 3rd of January, was bright and fine. From daybreak the occasional boom of great guns with distant strains of military music had been floating on the air, and by eleven o'clock, the vast Linden Alley was densely crowded with Berliners of every class and rank, waiting to greet their Emperor.—" This was the people's Congratulation Court," said the papers of the day, which thus describe the ceremonial which then took place within the walls of the Alte Schloss.

"About 11.30 the Crown Princess drove up to the grand entrance. She was greeted with enthusiastic cheers, which were renewed at sight of the Crown Prince and Prince Henry, who came immediately afterwards.[1] The Empress next arrived, and was similarly greeted, as her attendants assisted

[1] Prince William was at that time suffering from an attack of measles.

her to mount the stairs (the Empress is an invalid, and cannot move without help). The Grand Duke and Duchess of Baden followed, and then one by one drove up the splendid equipages of the representatives of all the European Courts.

"As twelve o'clock sounded, a ringing cheer ran up the whole length of the Linden Alley; the Emperor had come forth and entered his carriage. ... He looked quite fresh (*echt frisch*), happy and well, yet a shade of emotion overspread his genial face. He wore his General's uniform, with the ribbon and chain of the Order of the Black Eagle. The Empress was dressed in white; the Crown Princess entirely in dove colour, with a court train and bonnet to match. When the Emperor had alighted he gave his arm to his daughter-in-law, and walked stoutly up the long marble staircase without pausing. At the door of the Chapel Royal the Empress awaited him, when he conducted her to her chair, placed, with his own, in front of the altar. The deep tones of the "Salve" poured through the building, and then Dr. Kögel pronounced a discourse from the steps of the altar, in which he briefly reviewed the principal events of the Emperor's reign.

"The Emperor entered the White Saloon with the Crown Princess on his arm at one o'clock, the Empress accompanying him, supported by her son and her son-in-law. During the whole of the Reception which afterwards took place, the venerable Kaiser remained standing. . . It was affecting to behold him greeting his two trusty old servants, Prince Bismarck and Count von Moltke. He took each, in turn, by both hands, and kissed him on each cheek with visible emotion."

Of the illuminations which concluded this bright Sunday, I have spoken in a previous chapter, as well as of a subsequent celebration in England, when the Crown Princess came from Berlin in the month of May, to the Queen at the opening of the Colonial Exhibition. The Crown Prince was at that time recovering from a severe illness, but in June, when the Jubilee Art Exhibition was opened and a magnificent Greek Procession took place in Berlin, the Prince and Princess were both present.

The Prince has since then witnessed two impressive German festivals. One August day in 1886, he came with the Princess Victoria to the quiet, grey town of Baireuth, in the Franconian highlands. The air was then full of emotion and excitement, for we had gathered there from every quarter of the globe to enjoy Wagner's most spiritual, most impressive creation, and while we were listening, with bated breath, to the strains of "Parsifal," its composer's friend, that great maestro who was, of all others, the most closely bound to him, by family ties and artistic sympathies, was lying dead in the old town hard by. Three days previously,

Franz Liszt had passed away gently in the midst of all that was dearest to him. Immediately after his arrival at Baireuth, the Crown Prince sent a beautiful wreath to to be placed on the coffin of the great musician.

Shortly afterwards, the less solemn, but not less impressive commemoration of the quincentenary of the University at Heidelberg, claimed the interest and presence of the German Imperial Prince. Here his unbounded popularity was warmly recognized. On that evening when the stately ruins of the Castle were so magically illuminated, the Prince was making a circuit of them with his sister, the Grand Duchess of Baden, by his side, when a storm of huzzahs burst forth, which resounded again and again through those ancient walls and archways. The excellent speech made by the Prince at the banquet held on the succeeding day was quoted in all the German papers with words of praise.

As we were sitting amidst the deserted ruins of Heidelberg Castle one bright moonlight night in August—"its lights fled, its garlands dead, and all (as we supposed) but we departed "—suddenly a full burst of melody streamed out on the silent air. A chorus of men's voices rose up out of the cellar where, as it afterwards appeared, the concluding "Commerz"[1] of the students was then

[1] Answering to our college "Wine."

taking place. They sang Scheffel's Lied, "Behüt dich Gott," as only Germans can sing such a strain, and it seemed truly, to be a fitting *Vale* to the week's festivities.—"God guard thee!"—What better prayer can be breathed, be it for Imperial Prince or for simple citizen!

XIV.

ART AND INDUSTRY IN BERLIN.

> *"True art .. is an influence in the soul so heavenly, that it almost seems akin to grace. It is a worship as well as a theology. The temper of art is a temper of adoration."*
>
> FABER.

THE royal personages whose lives we have been following, are too warmly and practically concerned in the cause of education to limit their exertions for its spread within the narrow circle of their home life. From her own children's schoolroom, the Crown Princess betakes herself to the Pestalozzi-Fröbel House, to the schools for the industrial training of women, to the Victoria Lyceum, to the drawing classes in connection with the Museum of Industrial Art; bringing to each, in turn, the stimulus of her clear judgment and active sympathy.

"My wife understands everything," the Crown

Prince is reported to have once said. He, himself, may often be found perplexing and delighting the boys at the "Real," or Modern, Schools in Berlin, by odd and puzzling questions.—"One morning he had turned into the village school at Bornstedt. The postman just then came in and handed a telegram to the schoolmaster. To judge by the poor man's face, this contained bad news. The Prince insisted on knowing what it was.—'Your mother ill? Why, you must go at once to her!' —'But, sir, my class—my children?'—'Never mind, I will take them till the clergyman comes at eleven.' And the Prince did really attend to the school for a whole hour.—We have to do with a man who considers, with dear old Hesiod, that no work brings shame."

Another day an old college friend visited him to explain the working of a society recently set on foot for the employment of tramps.—"Stay, let me have my children in—they ought to know of such work as this," said the Prince; and then Pastor Bodelschwing told of all the sin and misery, the seeming hopelessness of the lives of the poor fellows who come to work at his stone quarries at Wilhelmsdorf, of the change in their countenances after even one hour of honest labour.—"Do not forget that I shall be anxious to know how your colony prospers," said the Prince to his friend at parting, "I trust it may be the precursor of many such in our country."

"Debarred by constitutional usage from all participation in the government of the empire, the Prince follows with growing interest the slow and gradual development of *self-government*, the greatest progressive work Germany has embarked upon since the days of Stein and Hardenberg. He trusts the people—he believes in their rightmindedness."

"Our Imperial Prince and Princess began their married life together under exceptionally fortunate conditions, both being equally concerned for the good of their fellow men, and for all that can promote the moral, intellectual, and material progress of the people.... The spirit of Christianity, as replacing the dead letter, religion, as distinguished from dogma, is the basis of all their educational theories. The poetic and artistic masterpieces of every period of the world's history excite their enthusiastic admiration. They are keenly alive to their refining and regenerating influence, and are eager to extend the benefits of the museums and national collections to the whole nation."

The Princess, as we know, is a productive artist. The Prince is also an excellent critic. When he made the Nile voyage, in the year 1869, it was in company with Lepsius, the great Egyptologist, who has succeeded in reproducing the daily life of the ancient Egyptians so marvellously within the walls of the Old Museum in Berlin. To him it was that the Prince remarked, when they visited the Museum of Antiquities at Cairo together—" I am converted now to the belief that this people (the ancient Egyptians) had a true—yes! even a sublime feeling for Art."

The explorations at Troy, at Olympia, and at Pergamon,[1] which have been so liberally supported by the imperial exchequer, claim the Prince's interest in an especial manner, from the fact that his tutor, Dr. Ernst Curtius, was one of their earliest promoters, and is almost unrivalled as a graphic exponent of the history of Greek art. The great frieze from the temple of Zeus at Pergamon, recently recovered from the dust of ages by the indefatigable efforts of Herr Humann, and conjured to Berlin by some process of modern magic, which suggests the lost arts of the pyramid builders, has been so skilfully pieced together, even in its temporary arrangement in the Old Museum, that he who runs may read its story. It is nobly conceived, and has been executed by the nameless artists of two thousand years ago, with strange, dramatic force. It represents the battle between the

[1] We are warned by modern German writers not to confound Pergamon, the royal city, with Pergamos, the citadel of Troy.

gods and the heroes. The heroes, or giants, part beast, part fish, part bird—symbolizing, may we not suppose, the lower animal nature?—are worsted in their struggle with the celestial powers, who stride over them victoriously, asserting the triumph of the nobler nature in man.[1] There is scarcely one of these colossal sandstone figures which is complete, but they have an enthusiastic old custodian who fills up the gaps by words, and seems to take a personal pride in each muscular limb, each fold of drapery. This intelligent person does not fail to tell English visitors of the value attached to these relics of Greek art by "the Crown Princely pair," a value which was proved this summer, when a splendid Greek procession was arranged, by their desire, in connection with the Jubilee Art Exhibition in the German capital. The classic train then wound its way through pretty gardens,—pausing occasionally by votive altars, where sacrifices were offered up,—to those temples of the Greek gods so skilfully reproduced from the fragments preserved by German enterprise.

The Museum of Industrial Art in the Königgrätzer Strasse is perhaps more representative of the artistic efforts of the Crown Prince and Princess than any other institution in Berlin. This noble building has grown up, almost stone by stone,

[1] This was, at least, the impression given to the present writer by this colossal specimen of early art.

under their direction. It is said that the Princess has chosen, if not designed, each of its sculptured groups, its metal castings, its fine mosaics and designs. Two thoughtful worthies guard its portals, Peter Vischer, the brave Nuremberg brass founder, seated at work on one of the shafts of his *magnum opus*, the shrine of St. Sebald ; and Hans Holbein the younger, pencil and block in hand, as if about to sketch his great Madonna of the Dresden Gallery. A band of life-sized figures, sculptured in sandstone, in high relief, runs round the whole of the lower portion of the building, where the eye can rest on it easily. These figures are grouped as working at the loom, the printing press, the potter's wheel, the student's desk, and beneath each group stands the name of the great mechanical inventor whose work it illustrates. Above this band are designs in terra cotta representing the handicrafts themselves, and the noble frieze which surmounts it all is of glass mosaic, wrought by Salviati of Venice, from drawings by Ewald and Edelschap. This frieze represents the great epochs of art and culture symbolized by single colossal female figures.

The museum has a vast central hall (used for loan collections) rising to the roof, and surrounded on two stories by suites of rooms opening into one another, their contents arranged chronologically, so that each art may be traced from its infancy to its maturity—occasionally from its decadence to its renaissance. The upper rooms are reached by a wide marble staircase, and open on a gallery running round the great hall. Each article is ticketed and fully described; but if more information is desired, the pleasant, intelligent attendant in charge of each room is always at hand to afford it. He seldom fails to tell English people of the constant visits paid to the museum by "the Frau Kronprinzessin," and to assure them that much of the fine ordering they must admire, is due to her clear mind and considerate care.

My last visit to this refreshing place was a very short one, for hard by were other institutions claiming interest both on account of their own value, and as exemplifying the kind of work which the Princess loves to promote. Leaving my friend, therefore, to copy a design for wood carving in connection with a "Home Arts" class, from a fine fourteenth century wall-cupboard, I passed by the huge Anthropological Museum, then in process of completion, and set off in search of No. 90 Königgrätzer Strasse. After the handsome Anhalt Railway Station is passed, the numbers follow each other tardily on a July morning in Berlin, and it was with a feeling of joy that at last I beheld the words "Victoria Stift" and "Lette Verein" looking me in the face. Turning in beneath an archway I then found myself in a quiet court, where a garden seat awaits the weary. This court is overlooked by long ranges of windows belonging to the technical school for women, and the boarding-house attached to it, both of which I hoped to see. At its further end is a restaurant, furnished with comfortable chairs, tables, newspapers, and most obliging attendants. Here stranger ladies, as well as the pupils and teachers belonging to the schools, can procure dinner or coffee at a modest rate. The pleasant lady who overlooks this department of the institution having indicated where I might present my credentials,[1] I presently found myself in the office of the secretary. This bright lady, who presides at a desk railed in from the inroads of the public, was beginning to describe the objects of the various affiliated societies which constitute the " Verein," when Frau Schepeler-Lette, the present representative of its founder, came in. I was welcomed by her in English, and with a reassuring friendliness.—" But," she said, after speaking of the work of the various schools, " you had better see for yourself what we are doing. Here is the house-mother of the Victoria Stift— our boarding-house—who will take you into all our departments. You will find evidence everywhere of the kind interest taken in our work by the Frau Kronprinzessin. Her support is most stimu-

[1] A letter of introduction to Frau Schepeler-Lette.

lating to us, and her help is always practical and valuable. . . . Fräulein Rüder speaks English," added she, as she turned to introduce a tall and graceful young lady, with such an expression of goodness in her brown eyes that one felt her name of " house-mother " to be singularly appropriate.

Saying that we had better begin at the foundation, this pleasant guide led the way to the basement, where the school for laundry work was pursuing its functions with much briskness and energy. Washing and ironing were here proceeding actively, as well as the "getting up" of fine *lingèrie* and lace, and spotless shirtfronts, under the vigilant eyes of professed laundresses. Thorough training in this work is given to girls of the servant class, while the daughters of well-to-do people frequently come here to learn those useful arts of clear-starching, lace washing, etc., which used not to be thought beneath the dignity of our great-grandmothers in England. Bonnes and nursery-governesses also attend these classes, and find a knowledge of such work a useful addition to their stock of capabilities. In order to help the funds of the institution, washing is done for families. One hundred and thirty-four girls were entered on the books as pupils of this branch of the Verein during the past year. The fee is fifteen shillings for a three months' course of instruction. As we wend our way up the stairs I am told that twenty-five free pupils, twenty-seven half-free, are paid for, in various departments of the schools, by the founders, namely, the Crown Princess, Herr Lette, the original founder, and a Frau Charlotte Stiepel, who bequeathed a sum of £3000 to the society in 1871 for the industrial training of the orphan daughters of officers and members of noble families.

Our next visit was to the office of Fräulein Anna Henning, the accomplished lady who manages the work of registering, and placing girls of all ranks in situations. Some idea may be formed of the labour necessitated by this branch of the establishment when we consider that in the course of its correspondence alone 6,495 letters were received, 6,012 written last year, and that 642 governesses, bonnes, Kindergarten teachers (77 of these), book-keepers, household servants, etc., were placed out during 1885. Fräulein Henning, who is fluent in English, told me much that was interesting in connection with her work, letting me peep also into her large and beautifully kept account books. There is no stated charge for this work of registration, but ladies who make use of the society are expected to become subscribers of at least three shillings a year to its funds.

A livelier scene presented itself on the next story, where the school of dressmaking is held in large, airy rooms. The lady who superintends this favourite branch of instruction has qualified for it herself by a special course of scientific and practical dressmaking, and seems to exercise a peculiarly gentle influence over the young girls under her tuition. Every one is very busy to-day; many are kneeling before those mute elegancies[1] which stand about the room so patiently, clad in graceful draperies, mysteriously folded, and adorned with their little occult puffings and puckerings, for to-morrow dresses will be finished and taken home for holiday wear. In an inner room stands an alarming black-board, squared into centimetres, on which segments of garments are portrayed, to be afterwards copied in white chalk on a broad, smooth deal table, before being cut out in paper. Finally, these patterns are cut out in miniature, and tucked neatly into the cunning pocket attached to a stout little blank book with which each pupil is provided, and which will be presently filled with dimensions, drawings, descriptions, etc., and produced as a test of proficiency at the end of the term.

A gay company of young milliners pursues a lighter branch of female adornment in the corresponding rooms, a story higher up. A "professed" *modiste* here directs the fashioning of caps and bonnets, babies' hoods, and grandmothers' "Mützen." Prentice hands are tried on

[1] Dress frames.

these last, and are promoted to *black* caps, we hear, when sufficiently clever in pleating up the soft white headdresses old ladies affect in the Fatherland. Just now the "wear" is evidently more juvenile. Hats abound, ready for the strand, for parents are about to carry off their little ones in the approaching holidays, to the islands of the Baltic, where they may imbibe salt breezes and ozone towards the work of the next school term.

Bright Indian cottons, too, are being drawn, and mysteriously puckered up, into those pretty, big hats and bonnets, which cost so little and are so cool and comfortable, while head-gear of more expensive material adorns many of the "dollies,"[1] which have their permanent abode here.

"You see," said Fräulein Rüder, "if one sister knows how to make the family hats and bonnets, the rest can have them for next to nothing." One hundred and ninety-seven pupils have attended the classes for dressmaking; ninety-six have attended the millinery classes, during the past year.

The corresponding rooms on the top story are the lightest and brightest of all. Here the best eyesight is needed for fine white work, beautiful marking, darning, etc., as well as for that artistic needlework which is now proceeding so briskly. Here you find bewitching samplers, filled with squares of open work, marking stitches, satin stitch,

[1] Milliner's blocks.

old German stitch—more fine stitches, indeed, than one has ever dreamt of before. These samplers can be bought, and would charm the hearts of some of our neat-handed English embroiderers. In an inner room, specimens of silk and gold embroidery may be seen and purchased. There are cutting-out departments, and the use of the sewing machine is also taught. Altogether, in the course of a year, two hundred and seventy pupils have been entered on the books in this department.—But we must not be beguiled into too long an inspection of the products of these deft German fingers, for much still remains to be seen.

The library, with its well-stocked shelves, and papers, and magazines, is close by. Both out-pupils and boarders can borrow books here at the rate of a halfpenny a week.—A wise insistence upon payments, however small, prevails in every portion of this institution.—The large general sitting-room is well furnished, and provided with a piano, on which any boarder may play for half an hour at a time; but if the instrument is needed for practising for professional purposes, and for some hours daily, a charge of eighteen-pence a month is made for its use. Here breakfast, and the morning and afternoon coffee, are served to boarders; dinner and supper are eaten at the restaurant. We are now in that part of the building devoted to the boarders of the Victoria Stift. Their cheerful rooms open upon a long corridor lined with wardrobes holding their clothes, and look on the quiet court before mentioned. We peeped into some of these tasteful little chambers, where the air was fresh, as windows stood open in obedience to a "polite request" hung up everywhere. Forty-five girls can be accommodated here, and the beds are generally filled by country pupils, attending the classes in the school in order to qualify themselves for earning an independent livelihood. For board and lodging, light in sitting-room, washing of bed-linen, and medical attendance, 15s. a week, or £3 5s. a month, is charged. A lady doctor attends for consultation on Mondays. There are many simple and salutary rules which tend to the well-being of pupils and of college alike, and the sympathy and loving care of the house-mother are extended to all these young boarders.

All the busy work I had seen so far, belongs to the industrial, or "Gewerbe," division of the institution. There is also a School of Art which attracts a large number of pupils, and which includes in its course freehand drawing, geometry, drawing from casts, architectural drawing, drawing of patterns and designs, flower painting, colouring, and lectures on the history of the fine arts. We found the pupils here busily engaged upon competition work, some of which seemed to be excellent. The silver medal presented by the Crown Princess is awarded, each term, to two or three pupils in each of the different branches of this school. The third division of the Verein, is the business, or "Handelsschule." Book-keeping and commercial correspondence, with French and English conversation, German, and geography, are taught here; but as the classes had just closed for the holidays, I did not see these embryo clerks at work. The reports of the usefulness of this branch of the school are very encouraging. Three of its pupils succeeded in gaining the Princess's silver medal for industry, efficiency, and good conduct, respectively, during the past year.

Gymnastics are taught by a lady during part of the year, at the Royal Military Gymnasium. There is a Victoria Bazaar, somewhat on the lines of our "Ladies' Work Society," in Sloane Street, under the patronage of the Princess Louise, where ladies' work of all kinds is sold for the benefit of the makers. There is a loan society,[1] which lends sums not exceeding £7 10s., at the rate of 3 per cent. interest, to women desirous of buying sewing machines, or other bread-winning appliances. Lastly, there is a school of cookery in connection with the restaurant. Over one hundred dinners are prepared here daily, and may be had

[1] The Lette Stiftung.

at the rate of sevenpence each, as contracted for by pupils and teachers; ninepence is charged for single dinners supplied to strangers. Seventy-two girls have qualified in cookery during the last year.

The foregoing sketch of the working of this excellent institution, is very meagre and inadequate. This Verein resembles no group of schools at home, I think, so may interest persons who are engaged in promoting the industrial training of women. I wish I could present to my readers a better picture of the pleasantness, the cheerful activities of the whole place, and convey to them some idea of the gentle influence which the ladies at the head of its different departments appear to exercise over the young girls under their charge. The practical help, the ever ready support they receive from the Princess, their "Protector,"[1] gives an impetus to the whole establishment—so these ladies say—while she suggests some of their best arrangements.

This is not the only institution which supplies proofs of her interest in the technical education of women. Another, and kindred establishment, intended to meet the wants of women of a class perhaps even more in need of that training which may fit them for becoming self-supporting, than are the pupils belonging to the Lette Verein, has been

[1] A pleasanter term than "Lady Patroness."

set on foot mainly by the exertions of the Crown Princess. I should like to give similar details of this "Home for Girls of the Higher Middle Classes,"[1] did space permit. This Home has to thank the Emperor, the Princess, and other members of the royal family, for substantial pecuniary help, and for—"That benevolent interest which is a spur to them to work energetically," as the report of its committee expresses it. It provides ladies who attend schools of art, or academies of music, or who go out as teachers, with a cheerful and home-like residence. It is also an educational establishment on similar lines to the "Lette Verein." The number of its pupils exceeds that of the kindred house, while the fees for instruction are lower. It is intended to benefit the daughters of professional men, government officials, officers, and merchants exclusively, and it affords special facilities to orphans, young childless widows, and destitute girls of the upper classes, who wish to qualify themselves for earning an independent living.

The large house in the Charlotten Strasse devoted to its use, is cheerful, handsome, and healthy, and the house-mother, Fräulein Toni Lütze, appears to possess the entire confidence of the large family confided to her care. She told me how bright had been the Christmas festival last year, when

[1] Heimathshaus für Töchter Höherer Stände.

the "Frau Kronprinzessin" had given to each pupil a large photograph of the Home, to preserve in memory of the days spent under its roof.

There is yet another institution in Berlin bearing the name of the Princess, the Victoria Lyceum, which has the higher culture of women for its object. This Lyceum affords lectures and classes to facilitate the study of special subjects. Girls whose schooling is supposed to be ended, as well as those who are still attending the High Schools, can benefit by these lectures. The Lyceum has been in existence for eighteen years, under the especial protection of the Crown Princess. Miss Archer, an Englishwoman, formerly governess to the Princess's children, was its first directress, a post now filled by Fräulein A. Cotta. Lectures are given by the first professors of Berlin in Greek, Latin, various branches of science, philosophy, modern languages, history, literature, the physiology of health, as well as on the history of art and music. Classes for modelling, painting, drawing, etc., are held. The recently-established centre for lectures in connection with King's College in Kensington, resembles this Lyceum in its course of instruction. It is needless to say that this institution claims the warmest interest of the Princess, who was, I believe, its original founder.

Miss Archer was also instrumental in carrying

out the idea of a Sanitary Association for house to house visiting of the poor, of which, in connection with the further work of the Princess, I hope to speak in the following chapter.

XV.

SERVANTS OF THE SICK AND POOR.

> "*It would be hard to find stronger evidence that the times we live in are better than the times past, than that young ladies of good social position, influenced by the high motives of religion and charity, give themselves to the work of nursing the sick poor.*"
>
> SPEECH OF SIR JAMES PAGET.

IN the year 1867, the thoughts of the Crown Princess were occupied by a subject which has always stirred her interest and sympathy in an especial manner. The experience of the short, but sanguinary, campaign of 1866, and a subsequent outbreak of cholera, had proved the existing nursing agencies of Germany to be inadequate to its needs, and the Princess then earnestly desired to see an efficient training school established in Berlin, where educated women might gain a thorough knowledge of the *science* of nursing.

The Princess could see that gentlewomen might earn a competent livelihood by following this noble profession while working beneficently amongst the poor, and she penned at that time the first of two important memorandums, a portion of which Fräulein Amelie Sohr has been permitted to embody in her book on women's work.

"Without doubt," said the Princess in 1867, "the best nurses would prove to be those who would combine the obedience of the Catholic sisterhoods with that more scientific and comprehensive training which has not, as yet, been obtained by any Sisters belonging to Orders. The Kaiserswerth Institution has, it is true, comprehended something of this object in its fundamental principles, but the education of its sisters is not sufficiently scientific. The establishment of a Nursing School is a most important project, and at present, just after the war, it might be carried into effect with the best results. Here, in Berlin, ladies might easily combine to obtain that efficient training which our existing hospitals could afford them until a special hospital and a Home might be created. When that was effected, our sisters could go forth to establish affiliated branches in connection with this central Home. When travelling for this purpose, as well as in their daily work, a distinguishing dress and badge should be worn. Periodical examinations would be held, and prizes for efficiency awarded.

Experience teaches us that without careful attention to apparently trivial matters, great ends are seldom attained. In sending out little missions to found schools, hospitals, etc., more especially in foreign countries, consists, in a great measure, the secret of the success of Kaiserswerth and similar institutions."

The outbreak of the great war in 1870 delayed the execution of this plan. Such agencies as then existed had to strain every nerve to meet the pressing needs of the hour. Her personal experience during the terrible winter of 1870–71, only confirmed the Princess in her conviction that more scientific training for women, in a vocation which, of all others, directs the womanly instincts into useful channels, was urgently needed in Germany.

In 1872 the Princess wrote a longer and more exhaustive memorandum on the subject which occupied her thoughts so anxiously. A few passages translated from this document may serve to illustrate still further her ideas on this important question. The Princess invited cultivated gentlewomen to join in the work, considering this to be one of the great requisites for its success— "The orphan daughters," she said, "of military men, government officials, etc., who have received a good scholastic education with gentle home nurture, would be especially fitted for this profession. They would receive a three years' theoretical and practical course of instruction, after entering the Home as probationers. At the end of this training they would be examined in hygiene and in natural science, as well as in the rudiments of surgery, anatomy, and medicine. They would then go through a course of monthly nursing, with the management of new-born infants. Proficiency and especial aptitude, together with a good general education, would qualify them for the posts of superintendents, and from these the matrons would be selected." After enlarging on the details of the scheme, the Princess concludes with the following words : " If ladies of position would give themselves to the organising and supervising of this work, it would prove an encouragement to the nurses, who would thus gain the assurance that they belonged to a society which was extending a loving and protecting arm over them. We should, however, create no Order; ours would be entirely free Samaritan work. Our nurses should be at liberty to obey the call of the sick and suffering any moment. More especially in cases of accident or sudden seizures, there would be no hindrance to their instant attendance. This service of love ought to be sufficient to open all hearts. With the best intentions in the world, sisters who are fettered by the rules and observances of particular religious Orders, cannot always obey the calls of humanity."

In confirmation of the far-seeing wisdom of these words, the writer may mention the case of a young relative living in the east of France, who last year engaged a sister from a neighbouring convent as monthly nurse. The duties of her Order obliged this nun to absent herself each morning at six o'clock, and at intervals again during the day, quite irrespective of the needs of the young mother and her first baby. This may, however, have been an exceptional case. Fräulein Sohr speaks with admiration of the good work done by the "Grey Sisters,—excellent women, who have been working noiselessly and devotedly for years in one district of Berlin, and who are beloved by poor and rich alike;" as well as of other nursing associations in the capital. These, she tells us, are by no means sufficient, however, to cope with the needs of its rapidly-increasing population.

While the Princess was thus striving to awaken the ladies of Germany to the importance of founding schools for skilled and unsectarian nursing, thanks to the exertions of Mrs. Dacre Craven who, when Miss Florence Lees, had assisted the Princess in the direction of her Field Lazareth at Hombourg, such a school was established in England. In the year 1875, Mr. William Rathbone, with the help of the Duke of Westminster and other gentlemen of note, and guided by the practical wisdom and large experience of Mrs.

Craven, founded the Metropolitan and National Association for Providing Trained Nurses for the Sick Poor.

As the oldest pupil of Miss Nightingale, Mrs. Craven may be said to represent our modern English school of practical and scientific nursing, while, as having been closely associated with the Crown Princess in this work, she may be called our English exponent of the theory of her Imperial Highness, that the influence of the "gentle" over the "simple,"—of cultivated, well-bred women over the debased and ignorant, is likely to bring about the best results.

Mrs. Craven had assured herself, by personal inspection of the nursing service in all our large towns, that no permanent improvement can be looked for in the houses and lives of our poorest classes from the ministrations of paid nurses of the servant class, and that this can only be effected through the personal work and influence of gentlewomen, who will bring discretion, fine tact, and enlarged sympathies, to their difficult task.

As exactly applying to the kindred work now established through the exertions of the Crown Princess in Berlin, I will quote a few sentences from a touching little record of work written by Mrs. Craven, prefacing them by her remarks on the nature of the work which these devoted women have to face in the cause of humanity:

"The occurrence of illness in a family of the poorer classes usually finds its members destitute of the commonest sick appliances, and ignorant of the simplest means of nursing. . . . Yet to send these patients into a hospital would be to break up the home altogether. . . . To set these poor people going again with a sound and clean house, as well as a sound body and mind, is 'worth acres of gifts and relief. This is depauperising them.' A district nurse must know how to purify the foul air without causing a draught; to dust without making a dust; to disinfect so as to prevent the reckless diffusion of disease."

Mrs. Craven's experience proved to her that nurses of the servant class would not, as a rule, undertake to remove dirt without proper appliances—"There's nothing to clean with"—they would say when it was suggested to them to freshen the patient's room. They considered that their hospital training, in qualifying them for dressing wounds, bandaging, etc., exempted them from doing "anything menial," by which they understood that cleansing and freshening of the patient and his room which go so far towards recovery; nor did it ever occur to them to look into the sanitary arrangements of the house or its water supply.

Mrs. Craven once visited a terrible case of fever.

The child, who had nursed a whole family, was now herself at death's door, lying on a hard, ill-made bed, her hair matted with dust and perspiration, her lips blackened with fever, her whole aspect neglected and ill-cared for.—" I could not resist turning to the nurse and saying, 'Do you think you could sweep up the room and make it a little fresher, while I see if I can make the child's bed more comfortable?' She coloured and said in an offended tone—" I never sweep patients' rooms, ma'am. Our lady superintendents do not expect their nurses to do anything menial.' I then suggested that I should sweep and dust while she attended to the patient. 'There's nothing to do for her, that I can see, but what her mother can do as well as I can,' she replied.— 'What nursing did you do for the rest of the family when they were so ill?' I asked.—'I gave them milk and beef tea, and sometimes lent them sheets, and helped Maggie (the sick child) to make the beds.'"

A typical case, showing what kind of work is done by the ladies of our Metropolitan Association, will also indicate what, according to the report now before me of a year's work in Berlin, the ladies of the Crown Princess's Victoria House are effecting there.

A clergyman had reported a bad case of scarlet fever to Mrs. Craven, when she and one of her nurses went at once to the house, in some mews in Bloomsbury. They found one child lying on the window seat—where she had asked to be carried—dead, the young mother, who had never before seen death, afraid to touch it. Two other children were almost in the last extremity.—" The window and every crevice by which air could get in was pasted up carefully; the bed stood behind the door, where no air could reach it. The floor was covered with strips of carpet; the window hung with thick curtains. We performed the last offices for the dead child, and then carefully sponged the two sick children between blankets, put on clean linen, and made the bed without moving them out of it, took precautions against bed sores, cleansed the mouth and ulcerated tonsils, and combed and arranged the hair. . . . We took down the curtains, took up the pieces of carpet and folded them ready for disinfection, prepared a disinfecting solution to wipe over the floor and for all utensils used by the sick children, showed the mother how to disinfect, and arranged for ventilating the room without creating a draught. . . ."

A district doctor said, speaking of the work of these ladies—" The careful disinfecting used and taught by them, always prevents fevers spreading beyond the family where it originates." Nurses on 'fever duty' perform quarantine, and do not visit other cases while attending fever patients.

... Wherever a nurse enters, order and cleanliness must enter with her. She must reform and recreate, as it were, the homes of the sick poor. These unfortunates often have lost the feeling of what it is to be clean. The district nurse has to show them their room clean for once, and to bring about this result with her own hands—to sweep and dust, empty and wash out all the appalling dirt and foulness, air and disinfect, rub the windows, sweep the fireplace, carry out and shake bits of old sacking and carpet, fetch fresh water, fill the kettle, wash the patient and the children, and make the bed. 'Every room thus cleaned has always been kept so. This is her glory; she found it a pig-sty, she left it a tidy room.'

"These results can only be attained by one who is content to be servant and teacher by turns, and has the tact needed to command the patient's entire confidence. In short, a woman of a higher stamp than will suffice for most other kinds of work is indispensable here."

"A woman with a badly diseased leg, who had been suffering agony from the mistaken treatment of a parish nurse, said, after the first visits of the district lady nurses—'Oh! what a different place you've made my room, and how comfortable you have made me! The first night after you came I hardly knew myself for the ease I was in, after having been nearly mad with the pain for so many nights. And as to what you've done to the room! Why, I just hope I'll be able *to keep it the same* when I get about again.'"

It is not surprising to hear that the Crown Princess has visited the Home in Bloomsbury Square with peculiar interest and pleasure.

Knowing how to express their sympathy with the happy celebration of the silver wedding of their Imperial Prince and Princess in the manner best calculated to give them pleasure, the good Berliners quietly collected a sum of 180,000 marks (£9,000) and presented it to them in 1883 for special application to the funds of the Victoria House and Nursing School, which had been established in the capital in 1881. A further sum of 820,000 marks (£41,000) was collected at the same time throughout the whole of Germany, and placed in the hands of the Prince and Princess for application to any benevolent purpose which might commend itself to their sympathy. From this a sum of 170,000 marks was taken, 2,000 was added by the Prince and Princess to the 118,000 collected in Berlin, and the total sum of £14,500 thus produced was at once applied to the endowment and maintenance of the work so dear to the heart of the Princess.—I have seen the original deed of gift of this money, at the house of a member of the Society for the Promotion of Health in the Home, signed in the large, clear characters of—"Friedrich Wilhelm, Kronprinz," and of—"Victoria, Kronprinzessin, Princess Royal of Great Britain and Ireland."

A German lady, Fräulein Fuhrman, was then sent to the Central Home of our Metropolitan and National Nursing Association, that, in accordance with their rules, her capabilities might be tested before she was sent to St. Thomas's Hospital for training in surgical and clinical nursing. When her course of instruction at the Hospital was completed, Fräulein Fuhrman returned to the Home in Bloomsbury Square for special training in nursing the sick poor in their own homes, in obstetric cases and the management of new-born infants, in the treatment of scarlet fever, and in the principles and practice of the science of disinfecting.

When Fräulein Fuhrman returned to Berlin, and the Committee of the Victoria House had become aware of the value of her training, she was placed in charge of the nursing of the magnificent "Stadt Hospital," just reorganized under the personal direction of the Crown Princess. This institution, from its situation in a park, well out of the smoke of the city, is referred to in our introductory chapter as the Friedrichshain Hospital. It is built in many detached blocks; its wards are large and admirably arranged; it has a splendid medical and surgical staff; and its nurses are ladies, whose gentle looks and tones carry comfort to all who receive their ministrations.

While the earlier chapters of this book have been going through the press, I have heard of a delightful evening entertainment given to the sixty lady nurses of the Victoria House attached to this Hospital, spoken of by the Crown Princess, who was then present, as a most interesting and enjoyable meeting.

Fräulein von Boltenstern, the present superintendent of the nurses for the sick poor in Berlin, who resides at the Victoria House, 16, Steinmetzer-Sternstrasse, has also been trained at the Central Home of the Metropolitan and National Association, under the direction of Mrs. Dacre Craven, her hospital training having been received at the Royal Infirmary in Edinburgh. When you look into the gentle, peaceful countenance of this sweet young lady you may read there the traces of her noble work. Those who come under her influence may well be encouraged to "go and do likewise."

The Society for the Promotion of Health in the Home[1] has two other branches besides the one I have tried to describe. In the year 1878, Miss Archer, formerly governess to the children of the Crown Princess, then directress of the Victoria Lyceum in Berlin, made an urgent appeal to the ladies and gentlemen of the capital to form a society for house-to-house visiting of the poor, for

[1] Häusliche Gesundheit.

their instruction in household management, and their encouragement in industry and cleanliness. It was proposed to teach simple cookery, the care and management of young children, and to impart to them such ideas of beauty and grace as might tend to the growth of cheerfulness in the spirit and faith in the heart.—" The home," said Miss Archer, " is of infinitely greater importance to working men than to those who can afford other resources. It is the basis of their moral, as well as of their physical, health."

The Crown Princess is the protector, as she was the originator, of this society, which is now in full activity in Berlin.—" Not only has she afforded us much practical help and advice, we have to thank her for some of our fundamental principles," say the committee in their yearly report of their work.

The third branch of this association is that which gives a country holiday to city children, and which enables them, when needing it, to visit convalescent homes. For many years past, societies have existed all over the Fatherland for giving fresh air to the little pale-faced children of the great towns. Berlin is the head-quarters of these different societies, and the Crown Princess is their protector.

When the sea or the mountains are within easy reach, it is not hard to place out these little holiday folk; but, to quote from Fräulein Sohr—"All round Berlin the country is flat, sandy, and insalubrious, and it had been difficult to find good air and fresh water for our city children until the matter was taken up by our warm-hearted protector, the Crown Princess. She, by her influence, and with the co-operation of the railway companies, has opened the way for them to distant sea-side localities. She has herself given a happy holiday for weeks together to these little ones, at her farm-house at Bornstedt, amongst green meadows and peaceful streams. Let us peep in and see how one of these little "colonies" fared under the care of a royal hostess.

"They could play all the day long in the wide green fields, gleaning a harvest of pretty flowers, to be carried home and treasured as relics. They might even gather the fruit, and drink the sweet frothing milk which they saw streaming into the milking pails. They could stretch their thin little limbs in the baths, built out into the broad river. They might float on this river in delightful boats. . . . Up to the hour of their departure, when the evening meal was spread on the green sward for them, as well as for a second little colony from a neighbouring village, the loving kindness of the Princess was as a warm, protecting arm round about them. . . .

"You find these 'city mites' in many of our

country districts now-a-days, singing aloud and playing with the rosy village children. How good the noon-day meal tastes after a whole morning in the woods and fields! The sweet, clean rooms, the kindly human beings, the flowers, the birds, the friendly domestic animals—how much all this will give them to think of through the long winter in the murky town! To most of these children their three weeks' country holiday thus becomes a 'joy for ever.'

"Here a little troop comes pattering in beneath the great stone archway leading into an old-fashioned town. The workman sits outside his cottage door, plying his trade; the house-mother is carrying her 'wash' to spread it on the green meadow at the back of the house; the children are watering the cabbages and roses, growing in friendly proximity, within the bounds of the little garden. All nod, and smile, as the troop of city children pass by. Presently, when the sun is getting low, fathers and mothers, with their little ones at their hands, come out to climb the hill leading up to the castle hard by. Here they find the small townsfolk once more. A kind man has just been showing them a portrait, in one of the rooms of the castle, which has looked down upon them with wise, far-seeing eyes, for this is Reinsberg, where the great 'Father Fritz'[1] used to live when he

[1] Frederick the Great.

was Crown Prince Fritz—' the prettiest, vividest of little boys.' — The great King will henceforth be a living reality to these children; and thus a page of their national history gets woven in with the happy memories of their summer holiday."

LITTLE ARCHITECTS.

XVI.

THE CHILD'S GARDEN AND ITS PROMOTERS.

> "... Give them (children) not only noble teachings, but noble teachers."
> RUSKIN.

"KINDERGARTENS—Kindergartens for the children of our poorest classes—are what we have to look to for the regeneration of the world," said a clever Englishwoman to me lately.—"If we could spend more care, and thought, and love, on the earliest years of our helpless infant population, if their first impulses could be directed into wholesome channels,"—I said to myself, as I pondered her words—"might we not, indeed, in time hope to see much of our crime, and a great deal of our pauperism, abolished?"

Within the limits of a concluding chapter it is impossible to do more than suggest what that educational system, originated by the Swiss Pestalozzi, and completed by the German Fröbel, may one day signify to unborn generations.

The "child's garden" was so called by Fröbel to express his conviction that the human plant ought to be assisted to unfold itself naturally, gradually, mind and body growing and developing *from within*, and in the soil and atmosphere most conducive to its health. "The child," he said, "must be helped to produce what is within it." It must not be treated, to use Carlyle's expressive figure, "like a passive pitcher to be pumped into."[1] From the first stirrings of its mind and activities, the child ought to be considered a creative being, and its creative powers trained accordingly.—"A child," said Rousseau, "forgets what it has been shown; it never forgets what it has *made*." "A child," said Fröbel, "should neither learn nor work consciously; it should only play;" and so he provided children with playthings, or "gifts," which afford that play *with a result* which gives little children the greatest enjoyment, as all who watch them closely will observe.

Fröbel's gifts can be seen, collected and arranged in their order and sequence, with those of Pestalozzi, at Zurich, in that small museum, called the "Pestalozzi Stübchen," opened, in memory of their philanthropic townsman, by his admirers, and the "grateful people" of Switzerland. With the works of the older reformer are very rightly placed specimens of Fröbel's philosophical play-

[1] Referring to the recipients of Coleridge's eloquence.

things. Here we find the sphere, or ball; the cylinder, or hollow ball; the cube, or brick, with sticks, paper, peas, and sections of circles. These simple materials afford the means of producing endless progressive combinations, based on a deeply scientific principle, thought out by Fröbel during years of study and experiment, and tending to the unconscious development of the child's latent faculties. The employment of these gifts should, however, be guided by educated, intelligent, and sympathetic women, so that while the little hands are growing deft and supple, the eye may become accurate, the ideas clear and correct. An accurate perception of outward things leads to truthfulness in word and deed; while, as the beauties of creation are gradually revealed to the child, its thoughts and aspirations are raised to the Eternal Source of all blessings.

In Fröbel's Kindergartens children live in an atmosphere of love. The women who devote themselves to interpreting "the first intuitive utterances of the child's nature"—to quote from the Baroness Marenholz von Bülow—" cultivate motives, instead of ordering conduct. They open the eyes of the child to the perception of beauty and goodness, and so lead the heart up to God, instead of by teaching catechisms. . . The educational mission to which Fröbel calls women . . must appeal directly to that part of their nature which produces the loveliest results. . Whilst the child's soul is revealing itself to the mother, her own soul is opening out. . A place has been given to her in the world, where she has the highest duties to fulfil towards a growing human being. Her own worth and dignity are called forth; her heart is turned towards God, under whose eye, and according to whose will she has to fulfil her office of priest to her child's soul. . . All women may thus be raised to the dignity of spiritual mothers and educators of the human race. . . The highest earthly love is the love of humanity, and this must be the inspiration of women as guides of childhood. . . This, the high motive enabling them to call out and to foster the divine spark latent in every child."

This writer dwells, further, on the increasing necessity for the *intelligent training* of the working man, now that improved mechanical invention is always lessening the demand for the mere *human machine*, or mechanical worker. Those who have dealings with the poor in our great cities, find the unskilled labourer an almost hopeless client in these days.

The spread of technical education is happily occupying all thoughtful minds at present, and what better preparation can we find for the work of the technical school than Fröbel's Kindergarten? We need no assurance that children who bring observant eyes, nimble fingers, and awakened minds to school, will leave those who have had no preliminary training far behind in the race. Children trained in Kindergartens learn also to love work. The instinct for work is born with us all, and we find that a child supplied with plenty of occupation is seldom "naughty." Dr. Watts's well-known axiom, and its more recent version—

> "Satan still some mischief finds
> With which he tickles idle minds,"

go to the root of the matter. It seems to me that no sadder doctrine can be preached than that work is a curse. It is our best blessing. "Working man is a noble title for any human being," said Frederick Robertson. This is a doctrine which the Hohenzollern race fully recognizes. With them it is a family law that the heir to the throne should learn a handicraft—" For work shameth no man," say they, "but is, on the contrary, the noblest pillar of the State."—To give to work that intelligent value which will make it more to the mechanic than a mere means of earning daily bread, is to enrich his life and take the sting from poverty.

Many persons have heard of Pestalozzi and his

educational system, but of Fröbel less is known in England. His autobiography has just been translated into English, and to that interesting little book I refer those who wish to know the details of his early life, and of his efforts to discover a method of genuine education. His childhood was embittered by the harsh suspicion of his stepmother, and the rigid, puritanical rule of his father—the learned and energetic pastor of a large district in the Thuringian Forest. The conditions of his life were changed when, at ten years of age, his mother's brother, a clergyman of a mild and benevolent disposition holding an office in the Lutheran Church corresponding to that of our Archdeacon, took the boy to live with him, and sent him to the grammar school in the little town of Stadt-Ilm. Here he was led to contrast the different influence of two good men, and to see the value of that gentle, loving system, which became in after years the ground-work of all his own schemes for the training of the young. After some years spent in studying land-surveying, forestry, etc., he was able to place himself for a year and a half at the University of Jena, where two of his brothers had already studied. After a further interval of two years, during which time he filled the post of actuary to the Forestry department of the Episcopal State of Bamberg, and afterwards that of agent to two large estates successively, he formed a friendship with the rector of a model school recently opened at Frankfort-on-the-Maine. This friend, a former pupil of Pestalozzi, offered him a tutorship in his school, while he imbued him with a desire to see the Swiss philanthropist and his great establishment at Yverdon, on the lake of Neuchâtel.—From a visit of two weeks' duration resulted a subsequent residence of two years at Yverdon.—Fröbel meanwhile became tutor to the sons of a Frankfort gentleman, stipulating that the children should be placed under his sole charge, and in the country. In training these little boys he already pursued the natural method, but feeling that more experience was needed, he persuaded their parents to allow him to take his pupils to Yverdon, where he resided with them for two years. While he found much that was admirable in Pestalozzi's system, and the older man's genial and inspiring personality filled him with enthusiasm, there were points where he differed from his master, and he quitted Yverdon with a determination to develop the methods he had now studied exhaustively still further. He proceeded to Göttingen, where he studied hard for two years, feeling the need of more classical and scientific knowledge. He afterwards took the post of superintendent in the mineralogical department of the Berlin Museum, and here was led to speculate still further on the nature and development of man, while studying crystals, in connection with geometrical forms, and assisted also by his constant pursuit of botany. After many preliminary experiments, he finally opened his " Universal German Educational Institution," at Griesheim, on the Ilm, in Thuringia, in the year 1816, his five nephews forming the nucleus from which a large school grew up by degrees.

In 1817 two friends joined Fröbel who had been his comrades in Lützow's regiment of Chasseurs during the campaign of 1813.[1] These men gave themselves, with life-long devotion, to the promotion of the new system of education. One of them indeed became to Fröbel what Aaron was to Moses, and continued to carry on the great work after the death of his master in 1852.—In 1817 the parent Institution was removed to Keilhau, near Griesheim. In 1818 Fröbel married Frau Henriette Hofmeister, an accomplished and devoted lady who joined in all his schemes with heart and soul, sharing his hard work, cheering him under many discouragements, as his faithful helpmate for a period of twenty-one years.

[1] Theodore Körner, the author of "Lützow's Wilde Jagd," so popular as set to music by the Germans, belonged to this regiment.

Herr Barop, one of Fröbel's disciples, describes a walk taken in his company in the year 1837, when he had just succeeded in establishing a large educational establishment for little children at Blankenburg, two hours distant from Keilhau.— "'Oh! if only I could think of a suitable name for my youngest born!'[1] he kept repeating, as we walked on, looking down on Blankenburg, lying in the valley below us. Suddenly he stood still, as if rooted to the spot, and his eyes assumed a wonderful, almost refulgent, brilliancy. Then he shouted to the mountains, so that it was borne forth on the winds of heaven—"Eurêka!—I have it!—KINDERGARTEN shall be the name of my new Institution!'"

The later years of Fröbel's life were cheered by the help and sympathy of many pupils and disciples. One of these, the Baroness Marenholz von Bülow, influenced the Duke of Saxe Weimar to bestow one of his country seats upon him to be converted into a training college. This lady, whose excellent books have been already quoted, has worked unceasingly during the last thirty years for the spread of Fröbel's system. In the year 1867 she founded a Kindergarten in Berlin, the direction of which came into the hands of a great-niece and pupil of Fröbel's, in the year 1871.

Fräulein Henriette Breymann, inspired by the

[1] Many orphanages and schools had been founded by the friends in the course of the previous twenty years.

lofty aims and practical wisdom of her revered master, had established a girls' institute and Kindergarten at Watsum, near Wolfenbüttel, in the Duchy of Brunswick. The Breymann Institute was very successful, but its founder was induced to leave it in 1871 to become the wife of Herr Karl Schrader, now a member of the German Reichstag, and well known for his warm interest in the philanthropic work of Berlin. On coming to reside in the capital, Frau Schrader soon found scope for her energies in the furtherance of that educational work which is so dear to her heart. She has devoted herself with untiring energy to the further development of the existing Kindergarten, the founder of which now resides in Dresden. To ensure a permanent home for this infant community, as well as for many other kindred institutions, Herr Schrader has purchased that large house in the Steinmetzerstrasse, where the affiliated schools for pupils and teachers are now so happily located. In 1874 Fräulein Annette Hamminck Schepel, one of the best pupils of the Breymann Institution, came to Berlin to take the management of these schools, as resident directress. The friends are carrying on their good work in the fullest sympathy, and the Pestalozzi-Fröbel House goes on its way rejoicing, under their fostering care, and with the constant sympathy and support of its exalted protector, the Crown Princess.

With the same earnestness and ability which characterize all her work for the people, the Princess assists all the branches of this Kindergarten, which has to thank her for many of its best additions and arrangements. Her visits are frequent, her advice and encouragement are stimulating alike to teachers and to pupils. An instance of the quick perception with which she is gifted was told me by a former pupil of Frau Schrader's, now conducting a Kindergarten in Scotland. One wintry day the Princess came to visit the schools when suffering from a severe cold, and obliged to wear two veils; yet, as she passed through a small room which one of the young teachers was about to paper, the Princess observed that the girl was about to put a long strip of the paper on with the pattern upside down. She went up to her, took it out of her hands, and quietly turned it.

As the efficient training of teachers is one of the first requisites for the success of the new method of infant training, a school for Kindergärtnerinnen forms an important branch of the useful work of the establishment in the Steinmetzerstrasse. The training received there also fits young girls, in an especial manner, for becoming nursery governesses, bonnes, and mothers' helps. Pupils have come here from England and from Scotland, and are now spreading the benefits of the system studied under the inspiring influence of Frau Schrader and Fräulein Schepel, in their native land. Many a young Scottish mother in a border town well known to the writer blesses the day when a gentle "Auntie" opened her Fröbel-House in their midst, and provided a wholesome outlet for the energies of little "naughty boys," hitherto a despair to nurses. Many sturdy little fellows, who had merely suffered from "*les défaux de leurs qualités*"—the defects of their good qualities—are becoming rapidly "as good as gold," I hear.—Two such honest little lads, natives of the north of Ireland, had once been incarcerated in a visitor's room, for dire misdeeds.—" Boys," whispered an anxious little sister through the keyhole, " boys, are you *good now?*"—" No, Mary; we're badder than ever we were!"—" Oh-h-h-h-h! what *have* you done?" "Mary, we've broke ze jug and basin!"—Thus did they exemplify Fröbel's dictum that if nothing is provided to be *made*, something will be sure to be destroyed.

But it is not for little people whose parents possess " visitors' rooms " that the Pestalozzi-Fröbel House in Berlin exists. Some of its pupils, in the four divisions of the infant school, are only too glad to receive a penny, or halfpenny, dinner from the school of cookery upstairs, for their parents are out at work all the day. As a rule, about fifty children dine here every day, when they set out the soup, etc., for themselves, and also wash up spoons and mugs, under direction. This school of cookery was founded at the suggestion of the Crown Princess; the Princess Victoria was its first pupil; yet it is by no means intended for young ladies of the "upper ten" exclusively. It is filled with the same bright, genial spirit which pervades the children's domain. Here we may find a merry company of young ladies rolling paste, and whipping eggs, and mixing, and stirring savoury compounds, three times weekly, under a clever instructress. Combined with the practical work, are lectures on household economy, exemplified by neat rows of ticketed jars holding all sorts of grains, spices, dried vegetables, etc., etc., their prices and qualities set forth, with notes on their uses, and the quantities needed for each dish. The trim shelves and cupboards on which stands this orderly array recall the description given by Mrs. Dacre Craven of the store-room attached to the Field Lazareth of the Crown Princess at Hombourg. It has long been the excellent custom of young ladies of the *haute noblesse* in Germany to graduate in cookery. The crowning test, before marriage, of efficiency in this art used to be—in one family of charming daughters, at all events, well known to the writer—the unaided preparation of a whole German dinner of many courses, of which the bridegroom-elect was invited to partake. Not long since, this ordeal was described to me, the Baroness expressing her thankfulness for the practical knowledge, thus gained, which had proved so useful, afterwards, in the direction of a large house.

Another important addition to the effective usefulness of the Pestalozzi-Fröbel House is due also to the Crown Princess. Always thoughtful of the health of the people, she suggested that baths should be arranged for the children, where every child can be well scrubbed with soap and hot water at the cost of a halfpenny. These little payments are a wise and beneficent part of the whole system. The baths given on Fridays and Saturdays, are under the personal direction of Fräulein Annette Schepel, and are doubly beneficial, as serving to train young girls of the servant class in the skilful handling of children, of which so often young nursery maids and mothers are ignorant.[1] The bath, too, is a source of much glee, as well as a pleasant tie between the little ones and the young girls of the establishment. The healthy looks of the children speak well for this wholesome application of " sweet soap and water."

There are generally from twenty to thirty young girls receiving training in the Pestalozzi-Fröbel House which will qualify them for earning

[1] I know of one instance, at least, of injury for life being sustained by a child from the careless handling of a nurse when bathing it.

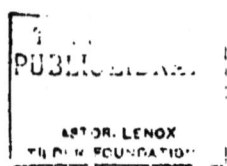

THE BATH-ROOM.

an honourable and useful living. Of these there are two divisions, in the first are girls of the upper or middle class, studying to become teachers of Kindergartens, helps to the mother, or her substitute, in some cases to be wives and mothers themselves.—The education of *mothers* was one of Fröbel's great aims.—Frau Schrader gives addresses on the fundamental principles of their duties to these girls, while other ladies instruct them in special subjects. The second class, comprising bonnes, nursery governesses, etc., are trained by Fräulein Schepel, who is often applied to by the matrons of Berlin to supply nurses from her gently drilled corps of capables.

The intermediate, or Vermittelung, classes, intended to bridge over the interval between the Kindergarten and the ordinary school, also find shelter under this comprehensive roof. Regular book-learning and lessons are here commenced, and are combined with industrial occupations. Here the free and happy little human plant gets trained to longer hours and drier work, work which, however, is made more intelligible than in most ordinary schools.

Little companies of girls—girls from ten to twelve years of age—may be seen of an afternoon carrying portions of the family wardrobe to a well-warmed room in this large house, for mending purposes, in connection with the " Patching and

Darning " branch of the Society for the promotion of Health and Domestic Economy, which holds its committee meetings here. These children sit together and sing, while repairing their own or their mothers' and sisters' garments.

Yet another addition to this busy home has been made at the suggestion of the Crown Princess. The rooms on its top story have recently been furnished as a Home for young women of the working classes, where they can live comfortably for a payment of from ten to fifteen shillings monthly, made by themselves when it is possible, when they are very poor, by charitable persons who may be interested in them. Their welfare is excellently looked after by a resident lady. Their meals, when required, are supplied from the cooking school in the same building.

There is yet another beneficent branch of this excellent establishment which must not be forgotten—the Victoria House, where Fräulein von Boltenstern and the ladies devoted like herself to the care of the sick poor in their own homes reside. This is in the garden wing of No. 16, Steinmetzerstrasse, which thus contains an epitome of the physical, the mental, and the moral, regenerative energies and activities of the city of Berlin.

XVII.

THE PESTALOZZI-FRÖBEL HOUSE IN SUMMER AND IN WINTER.

> "*Moral education is summed up when the creature has been made to do its work with delight and thoroughly.*"
> FORS CLAVIGERA.

IT was with a pleasant prevision of good things to come that we crossed the flagged entrance-hall of No. 16, Steinmetzerstrasse one early morning in last July. The cheerful little world contained within its precincts was now no longer a *terra incognita*, as it had been when we stood outside its hospitable doors six months previously. Letters of introduction from that Scotch friend before alluded to had ensured our kind reception on that occasion, and we were now returning as friends, to renew the impressions then obtained.

The young portress gave us a smiling welcome, and showed us into the ante-room, draped with small hats and jackets, and furnished with washing apparatus, which now seemed quite familiar to us.

Here a motherly little person of six, or so, was tidying up a smaller brother with much cheerfulness and decision. A chorus of " Tante ! Tante ! " could be heard drawing nearer, and presently Tante Annette Hamminck Schepel appeared, quite hung round with children. Her kind, wise face looked down smilingly on a rosy, eager petitioner as she was saying—" Yes, yes, if there is any, thou canst have some, my child.—They are begging for some bread to eat with our last bowl of curdled milk," explained kind Tante Annette, " we have had a cow, a real live cow, in our yard for the last month. We have been cutting grass for her, and visiting her, and she has given us milk and butter, and cream cheese. We are having our last churning to-day. If you like, we will visit the little butter-makers presently, but first you may be glad to see our haymakers. If so, we will go down to the garden." Behind the house is a good-sized piece of ground, walled in, and possessing a grass plot, where we find a cheerful company of little maids with pig-tails, and little men with close cropped heads, tossing baby hay with tiny rakes, to an accompaniment of song and laughter. Two pleasant young ladies are helping these farmer folk, and a third asks us to come and sit with her in a shady arbour where tiny posies are in process of arrangement, for before the breaking-up there is an interchange and carrying home of such pretty souvenirs. From our post of vantage, the various little crops, which are growing in strips all round by the wall, may be noted. Wheat and barley, rye and oats and Indian corn, may here be watched from seed to shoot, from stem to ear, from the mill to the oven. Potatoes and cabbages, peas and carrots, have been watered and wed, as well as those bright rims of cowslips and daisies and many another pretty flower, to be gathered to-day and tied up into little bunches, with the help of our kind companion. As the little ones come and go, we hear how Frau Schrader appoints an "object" round which all living interests may centre during each month of the year. This month, the dear cow has afforded endless delight and occupation. She has been moulded in clay, cut out in paper, outlined with needle and pencil. In April it was a violet; in December a fir-tree. I could recall a circle of eager listeners we had seen six months ago, to whom the Kindergärtnerin Marie was telling a true fairy tale of the woods and the fir apples, while many wonders were brought out of her magic basket, and many little fervent "*achs!*" and "*aber Tantes!*" accompanied her story. Here is a bit of the story of the fir-tree in Frau Schrader's own words as printed by her to help the young teachers.

"What is Marie bringing to-day to her three and four-year-old children? All eyes are upon a covered basket; it is filled with little fir branches; they are so green! they smell so fragrant! and yet the needles[1] prick a little too, though not so much but that we can take hold of them and make a pine forest out of them.—The children troop away to the kitchen and bring sand. The green twigs are planted firmly in this, so that they stand straight up. Then some one brings the Noah's Ark which was given last Christmas to the little ones. Wild beasts are living in the forest now! Marie's clever hands shape a little squirrel out of wax; it springs, with Marie's help, from tree to tree; it visits each child. Then, all of a sudden, it begins to snow; Marie has let a little shower of white paper, fall on the forest. What a stir this makes! Little master squirrel gets under a branch; all the bigger beasts crowd under the trees for shelter.

"Again, here are fir cones. The cleverest little fingers fill up the spaces between their scales with sand, and then stick them full of little flowers and leaves, which Marie has brought in her basket. The cone is cut level, so that it stands firmly, and when Tante Annette comes by, here is a fine, gay pyramid for her! The children make believe that

[1] The small spikes of the fir-tree are called fir-needles in Germany.

the cones are cows and horses, and build stables for them with bricks. A little carriage, made by bigger children out of paste-board, is brought from the toy cupboard. The cone horses are harnessed to it. . . . These little ones owe endless pleasures to the fir-tree. In the spring a fir sapling is planted in a pot, to grow into a little tree by next Christmas time. The little ones go off to the kitchen to fetch this pot, some sand, and watering cans. They bring all these to Marie; she calls them round her in a half circle, the smallest ones next to her, and shows them the little plant. They feel it, while she tells them its story, first making them gently see that they must be obedient, and not chatter too much, or else they will not all hear the story. She holds the stem while everybody adds a spadeful of sand to fill the pot. Then it is watered, and they watch it drinking in its first draught, by its thirsty little roots. Every class in the school has its own little tree— a foster-child to cherish lovingly through all the months of the year. Christmas comes, and then it stands, radiant with lights, the centre of all their joy. They see these little trees standing in the wide market-place. Where do they come from? Then it is that Marie tells them of the native home of the fir tree, of the rock and the mountain and the forest. How they would like to see those beautiful regions! Well, there is a place quite near; in the summer they shall see it. They will go to the Botanic Garden, where so many trees and flowers grow. . . . When the dear Christmas festival is coming the children help to deck the rooms. Then the story of the Christmas-eve is told, and pretty pictures are shown them. All the hope and expectation of the year finds its consecration in the story of the Christ-child, whose birth is then celebrated. . . . Richter's beautiful picture of the Angel of the Christmas-tree, bearing the Christ-child down from heaven, is shown to the little ones once a year, and it comes to them each Christmas with a new delight. . . . By tending animals and plants, watching natural objects, children are brought into a communion with life and nature, which cultivates their religious, poetic, and intellectual faculties."

Did space permit I would gladly translate more of Frau Schrader's simple and pretty descriptions of the months' objects.—But all this time while we have been watching the children tossing the hay and tying up little nosegays, the minutes are slipping away all too fast.—" Let us go upstairs and see the morning exercises," my companion says at last, so we proceed to the playroom, from whence a clapping of small hands and the clear tones of the teachers' voices are audible.

All the assembled infants are standing with

their eyes fixed on Tante Annette, her young assistants looking on. An active shooting out of short fat arms, a waving about of hands, a hopping and jumping, are proceeding with surprising vigour considering where the thermometer is standing to-day; but care is taken not to continue any one employment long enough to tire the infants. At a signal, all eyes are turned on Tante Annette, who then repeats, in her soft, clear voice, the words of the simple morning hymn. The children repeat them after her in a sweet infantine chorus, a young English pupil teacher, who is studying here, strikes a few chords on the piano, and then the little sinking and swelling song bursts forth, the thin little voices gently modulated, the words so heartfelt, and the old tune so sweet.

Some eyes were wet, I know, as these words were sung, which all, even the smallest, could comprehend:

> "Du lieber Gott, im Himmel du,
> Gabst mir auch diese Nacht
> So süssen Schlaf und gute Ruh,
> Hast mich so treu bewacht."

> " O ! Father dear, in heaven above,
> Thou gav'st me all the night
> Sweet sleep and rest, and still Thy love
> Doth watch and keep me right.

> "Du lieber Gott, ich danke dir
> Und deinen Engelein,
> Und bitte dich, O hilf du mir
> Stets gut und fromm zu sein." [*]

After a little reverent pause, each sturdy little creature takes its neighbour by both crossed hands, and off they all trample, in their little stout boots, under convoy of their young teachers, who each marshals her own eight or ten children to the spot where the play-work of the hour is to be found. Two or three business-like little trots carry back sundry low benches to the rooms to which they belong, and generally "tidy up"—work which it is thought a great privilege to share in.

It is scarcely possible within our exact limits to give our readers any adequate idea of what this play-work consists in, or of what qualities it is intended to develop in the little human plants it helps to nourish. Many excellent books describing the Kindergarten system and its "gifts," have been published in England, by the Fröbel Society, and to those I would refer all who may care to know more of this interesting system. Besides the work with cubes and spheres, sticks, clay, and

---

[*] O! Father dear, I thank Thee now,
And all thine angels too,
And pray that Thou wilt teach me how
To keep both good and true.

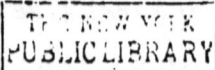

LITTLE LAUNDRESSES.

pasteboard and beads, these particular little housewives and husbandmen help in the various household avocations of the establishment. A special gift has been made to them of miniature brooms, dustpans, and tubs, with little smoothing irons and low tables, handy for "getting up" dolls' garments upon. They do some useful washing-up of plates and mugs, and scrubbing of wooden platters and spoons, used by themselves at their midday meal, and watch their teachers cleaning the lamps, etc. Presently we come upon the little churning party Fräulein Annette has spoken of. The churn is a mere baby one, with a churn-staff to match the short pairs of arms which dance it up and down by turns while the rest look on, and anxiously scan the yellow ring of butter which is gradually gathering circumference round it.

Tante Annette has, by this time, cut some substantial slices of the coveted rye bread which eager little hands then break up into a bowl of "our own cow's milk," and carry off for distribution. The children have put away their work, their toys, and are getting ready for the holiday breaking-up, helping each other, prettily, into hats and jackets.

And now Fräulein Schepel asks us to come with her to her bright sitting-room, in the heart of all these useful activities, open always to the children, as is also her kitchen. She speaks of this new system of infant training, and of its effect morally upon the little ones—of how it binds "each to each by natural piety"—of how it leads "from nature up to nature's God."—She speaks of the possibility of imparting the spirit of true religion, of reverence and love, without the aid of those formal catechisms which appeal so little to young children.—Love to God, love and helpfulness to parents and teachers, as well as to other little children, are the groundwork of all the efforts of these dear women.

As we sit together on her sofa, the kind faces of the Crown Prince and Princess look down upon us from the wall, and we recall the delightful Christmas gathering, which we were enabled, through Fräulein Annette's kind instrumentality, to enjoy six months ago. I ask whether she thinks it will be any breach of confidence, or of discretion, if I try to describe that bright evening as a fitting conclusion to the little account I am meditating of the People's Kindergarten. She cannot see that it will be so, and thus I am encouraged to tell my readers about the Christmas festival of 1885.

Triennially, this pleasant family party is held in the large rooms of one of the great modern schools of Berlin, and then it can include all fathers, mothers, brothers, and sisters of the little children.

This spacious building was filled with a cheerful hum of voices, and strains of martial music came

LITTLE MUSICIANS.

floating in at the doors of its large class-room, when we joined the ladies and gentlemen of the three committees for Häusliche Gesundheit there on the evening of the 23rd of December, 1885. Fräulein Annette Schepel was rehearsing a march, accompanied by her little band of drummers and trianglers, whose eyes looked bright, their little cheeks flushed, when we peeped into a small room to see this cheerful performance going on, as we proceeded upstairs. Already the benches, half filling the large upper room, were occupied by the families of the pupils, dressed in their Sunday best; and the tall tree, waiting patiently for its final illumination, was a thing of beauty as it stood draped in shining chains of gold and silver paper, bearing the cradled Christ-child on its topmost branch. Green garlands and pretty pictures decked the walls, while beneath the shelter of some pine branches spread a snowy landscape of cottages and mimic people all in sugared gingerbread, the gift of Frau von Rath, that lady who gave her beautiful house at Cologne for a hospital during the winter of 1870–71. Hundreds of fine gingerbread men and horsemen lurked close by, with the great heap of paper parcels which were by-and-bye to give such joy to little recipients. Young girls were standing, armed with long lighted tapers, ready to apply them at a moment's notice to the countless little candles on the tree, while ladies and gentlemen were saying pleasant words to the fathers and mothers waiting expectantly for the entrance of their little ones.

Then, a sound of wheels was heard, and suddenly the taper-bearers fell to their anxious work. Knowing the ways of those provoking little candles, I confess I had longed to see this business well begun for some time past. Before it was completed we could see a lady dressed in black standing alone in the open door-way and smiling in upon the busy scene. This gentle, girlish-looking, yet very dignified lady perceived with one glance of her clear, penetrating eyes that she had better *not* see just yet a little while.—I doubt whether any one but myself noticed her kind motive, for all were intent upon the tree.—The Princess, for she it was, then turned away for a minute to speak to Fräulein von Boltenstern,[1] beside whom I chanced to stand, and not till she was assured that all was ready, did she proceed to admire the pretty scene. Meanwhile, a tall, stately-looking officer had come in, accompanied by two slim daughters, their golden hair falling to their waists over their simple black dresses. As he held his spiked cap in his hand every one could recognize, by his wide brow, his bright blue eyes, his full, fair beard, that this was the Crown Prince.

His genial countenance beamed with pleasure as

[1] Superintendent of the District Nurses in Berlin.

he spoke to every one. At last he seated himself in an armchair, placed beside that which the Princess had been asked to occupy, while the little army of infants marched in, led by its commandante, Tante Annette, and her under officers. After bestowing many playful greetings on these small recruits as they trotted past, the royal hosts composed themselves to listen to the well-practised Christmas carol which soon burst from all those young lips in pretty modulated tones. To judge by the appreciation of the listeners, the children covered themselves with glory by this performance. Then one of the young teachers recited a short poem, with much dramatic expression. A gentleman next made a little speech, and then the Prince and Princess could proceed to the less formal part of the entertainment.

The little ones had looked a little shy, so far; but soon exclamations of delight and wonder were coming fast, as the fine gingerbread men found their way into short, fat arms.—" Mein Mann! Mein Mann!" wailed one very small person, who had lost his treasure; but he was quickly consoled when the Prince knew of his disaster. When, at last, a tall, soldierly form might be seen fairly kneeling down, the centre of a little crowd of infants, peeping into carefully-treasured paper parcels, holding up hands of well-feigned wonder, poking fun at some of the tiny creatures with the spike of a soldier's cap; when for a moment that soldier's cap covered a tempting little round yellow head close by, it seemed as if a true "Father Fritz" had indeed come amongst his children.

Meanwhile the Princess was busied in the work of distribution. When it was finished she could speak with the ladies and gentlemen who were helping the little ones to be happy. These kind people represented all the branches of those kindred benevolent associations for the improvement of the condition of the poor, in which the Princess takes an especial interest.

But now the well-practised march was about to be performed. With an absorbed and rather anxious look, Tante Annette seated herself at the piano, marshalling her little band of men and women around her, and the warlike strain burst forth. A score of soft, balled-up fists descended upon as many little jangling tambourines; short drumsticks came down with a fierce bump upon toy drums; the triangles chimed in, at carefully-counted intervals, each accompanied by an emphatic nod of a small head.—It was a pretty sight, and dear "Tante" might rest well content with her little children's performance.

When this gay little pageant had all faded away, and we found ourselves once more beneath the bright, silent stars, we could almost have fancied that the scene had been unreal—that the heart-stirring spectacle had been " of the stuff that dreams are made of"—so rarely is it that the world is privileged to see Princes in such true filial and paternal relations with the smallest and poorest of their people.

www.ingramcontent.com/pod-product-compliance
Lightning Source LLC
Chambersburg PA
CBHW022100230426
43672CB00008B/1229